In the *Image of God in the Parables*, Stephen Hiemstra teaches us about the person of Jesus, His teaching about the kingdom of God with the parables, and the church's founding on Pentecost by the Holy Spirit. In a world where humanity constantly seeks to understand itself apart from God, Stephen shows us that by discovering who God is in scripture, we discover who we are in Him. Our true identity will always be determined by God's divine nature and how He created us. Similar to other books in Stephen's series, this book is written in a devotional format with a reflection, prayers, and questions for study. The book will deepen your spiritual walk with the Lord as He continues to disciple us daily through His written word and many of life's experiences. I highly recommend this book and all the others Stephen has written.

Eric Teitelman
House of David Ministries

Image of God in the Parables introduces you to a different perspective of God that you might not have considered before, an intimate God that seeks you out to have a relationship of Creator with created. The questions at the end of each chapter help you think more deeply about what you have read. But the prayers are the crown jewel of each reflection. Deep and personal, these prayers help you align your heart with God's heart and will. Stephen Hiemstra truly takes you to a special place with God through his new book.

Nohemi Zerbi

Wanting to seek God in a deeper way helps us to relate to Him in a more effective way. It is precisely what this great book offers us. The possibility of finding through the parables a much deeper revelation of the essence of Jesus Christ. Stephen W Hiemstra helps us deepen the truths of the Kingdom of our beloved God.

Julio Martinez
Pastor, Shadai Phoenix

One of my passions is studying Scripture through varying lenses and topics. Consequently, I was pleased when Stephen W. Hiemstra asked me to review and endorse his book, The Image of God in the Parables. The title intrigued me, and the book is a lovely gift.

Stephen has structured a thought-provoking devotional that uses the parables to view five different aspects of the Image of God: mercy, grace, patience, love and faith. Each chapter concludes with a prayer as well as questions for reflection that solidify the focus of the chapter. Both of these encourage the reader to take in the content slowly and intentionally in order to thoroughly absorb key points.

As I read each chapter I frequently said Wow! out loud as Stephen presented God's character in a parable in new and fresh ways. I especially enjoyed the linguistic insights that add depth and richness to his insights.

The book concludes with some excellent insights about who God is not. Stephen reminds us that: "We can never fully comprehend God, but he invites us to try. When we do, the forms that lead us to him, like the parables and worship, no longer constrain us. They simply launch us into this new dimension available only through faith." Stephen has offered just such a new dimension in this lovely book.

Briane Pittman Kairns

Knowing we're made in the image of God is a source of comfort and awe, but all too often we don't dive below the surface of this amazing fact. In Image of God in the Parables, Stephen Hiemstra uncovers the image of God as Jesus taught in his parables. If you're eager to see the connection between our character and God's as Jesus shows us in his teachings about the kingdom of God, then this is the book for you.

Sarah Hamaker
Writer's coach
and author of *The Cold War Legacy* series

Bridging the gap between the academic and the personal, Hiemstra unites expert research and incisive practical observation. To his credit, his book would work as well as a text for a church Bible study as it would for a first-year seminary class study group. Clear, well-researched, and innovative, Hiemstra has produced an important work investigating the defining feature of humanity—the Image of God.

Paul Lauerman
Pastor, Centreville Presbyterian Church

"Jesus' parables are like the water offered to desert traveler lost, faint-hearted, and close to death." *The Image of God in the Parables* is a drink from the Living Water for the seeker who longs to quench his thirst for God in the arid desert of modern materialism. Dr. Hiemstra offers insight into God the Father in the parables of Jesus. He mines deeply in the culture and languages of the Old and New Testament and presents diamonds of spiritual treasures for those of us who long to understand more of Scripture.

Sharron Giambanco

OTHER BOOKS BY THE AUTHOR

Image of God Series:

Image of God in the Parables[2]

Image of the Holy Spirit and the Church

Image of God in the Person of Jesus

Christian Spirituality Series:

A Christian Guide to Spirituality[1]

Life in Tension

Called Along the Way[2]

Simple Faith

Living in Christ

Image and Illumination

Masquerade Series:[3]

Masquerade

The Detour

Christmas in Havana

Prayerbooks:

Everyday Prayers for Everyday People

Prayers[2]

Prayers of a Life in Tension

---

1 Also available in Spanish and German.
2 Also available in Spanish.
3 Screenplays have been adapted from these books.

IMAGE OF GOD IN THE PARABLES

Forgotten Path in Winter

IMAGE OF GOD IN THE PARABLES

Stephen W. Hiemstra

T2P

T2Pneuma Publishers LLC
Centreville, Virginia

IMAGE OF GOD IN THE PARABLES

Copyright © 2023 Stephen W. Hiemstra
Revised 2025
ISNI: 0000-0000-2902-8171, All rights reserved.

With the except of short excerpts used in articles and critical reviews, no part of this work may be reproduced, transmitted, or stored in any form whatsoever, printed or electronic, without prior written permission of the publisher.

T2Pneuma Publishers LLC
P.O. Box 230564, Centreville, Virginia 20120
www.T2Pneuma.com

Names: Hiemstra, Stephen W., author. Title: Image of God in the parables / Stephen W. Hiemstra. Series: Image of God. Description: Includes bibliographical references and index. | Centreville, VA: T2Pneuma Publishers LLC, 2023. Identifiers: LCCN: 2023905718 | ISBN: 978-1-942199-97-7 (paperback) | 978-1-942199-45-8 (KDP) | 978-1-942199-92-2 (epub). Subjects: LCSH Jesus Christ--Parables. | God--Christianity. | Christian life. | BISAC RELIGION / Christian Living / Devotional | RELIGION / Spirituality. Classification: LCC BT375.3 .H 2023 | DDC 226.8/06--dc23

Many thanks to my editor, Sarah Smith Hamaker, and to Jean Arnold and Donald Fairfairn, who offered comments.

All Scripture quotations, unless otherwise indicated, are taken from The Holy Bible, English Standard Version, Copyright © 2000; 2001 by Crossway Bibles, a division of Good News Publishers. Used by permission. All rights reserved.

Cover art by C. Hiemstra (2023), The Lost Sheep,
Used with Permission.
Cover by SWH

CONTENTS

PREFACE..ix

INTRODUCTION

The Face of God..3

Indirect Speech..8

Parable as Genre..13

Parables in a Postmodern Context................19

MERCY

The Good Samaritan..27

The Unforgiving Servant..................................33

The Barren Fig Tree..39

The Tax Collector and the Pharisee..............44

Applying Mercy... 49

GRACE

The Hidden Treasure..57

Lost Sheep..62

Sin as Sickness..68

Contending Grace... 72

Applying Grace..77

PATIENCE

Two Builders..83

The Sower..88

The Talents... 92

Ten Virgins... 97

Applying Patience... 102

LOVE

The Good Samaritan Revisited...................................111

The Two Brothers...117

The Friend at Midnight...122

The Dragnet.. 127

Applying Love...132

FAITH

The Rock..139

The Callous Judge.. 145

Pharisee and Tax Collector.. 150

The Physician..154

Applying Faith.. 159

CONCLUSION

Who God is Not..165

Image of God..170

REFERENCES...177

SCRIPTURAL INDEX..183

ABOUT THE AUTHOR.. 187

PREFACE

The LORD passed before him and proclaimed,

The LORD, the LORD, a God merciful

and gracious, slow to anger,

and abounding in steadfast love and faithfulness.

(Exod 34:6)

Our image of God reveals not only God's character, but our own. Jesus' parables reveal a God who is intentionally available to those who seek him. They invite the listener to enter the narrative and engage with God one-on-one to expand our understanding of faith and of ourselves.

The image of God in the New Testament takes at least three forms: The person of Jesus, Jesus' teaching about the kingdom of God with the parables, and the founding of the church on Pentecost by the Holy Spirit. This is a Trinitarian revelation of God, not by analytical description, but through word pictures. In this book I will focus on the image of God the Father found in the parables.

The authenticity of the parables as Jesus' own words is seldom questioned, in part, because Jesus' parables are unique, a genre unto themselves, but not a typical genre. A typical genre might adhere to a particular structure or story form, but not a parable. The parables distinguish themselves by inviting the hearer to participate in the story and requiring a response to the call to faith, many times without explicitly mentioning God.

This invitation to enter God's presence is unexpected and contrary to our experience. The narrative is more than the sum of the parts, like an Easter sunrise that transforms everything else. The freshness of the event surprises, even taunts us, to see everything new. It's like climbing the mountain to discover that you live on an island, but the good news is that on the horizon is a whole new world accessible through faith. Old limits no longer apply. God's transcendence works this way, and Jesus' parables provide a path to experiencing it.

Circumlocutions

Explicit in some parables and implicit in others are the words: The kingdom of God is like… Because the covenantal name of God, YHWH, is sacred in Jewish thought, the Bible uses numerous circumlocutions—indirect references—for God's name. The most common circumlocution is Lord, which in Hebrew is Adoni. Another common circumlocution is The Name, which in Hebrew is *Shema*.

The use of circumlocutions, indirect speech, like poetry, is most common in repressive societies. Jesus began speaking in parables after the Pharisees began to plot against him (Matt 12–13).

New Testament references to the Kingdom of God (Mark, Luke) or the Kingdom of Heaven (Matthew) are circumlocutions for the name of God. Almost all of Jesus' parables refer to the kingdom of God, while rabbinic parables typically elucidate a passage of scripture (Blomberg 2012, 77).

God's Self-Revelation

Because we are created in the image of God (Gen 1:27), it is important that we understand what God's image implies. After the second giving of the Ten Commandments, Moses is given a description in Exodus 34:6, cited earlier, of who God is that is repeated throughout the Old Testament (e.g. Ps 86:15, 103:8; Joel 2:13; and Jonah 4:2).

This latter reference is interesting because Jesus described his mission in these words: "For as Jonah became a sign to the people of Nineveh, so will the Son of Man be to this generation." (Luke 11:30) Because Jesus knew the story of Jonah, he clearly knew Exodus 34:6 for Jonah's reason for running away from Nineveh hinged on it: "That is why I made haste to flee to Tarshish; for I knew that you are a gracious God and merciful, slow to anger and abounding in steadfast love, and relenting from disaster." (Jonah 4:2). Jonah hated the Ninevites and refused to preach God's forgiveness to them because he knew God would forgive them if they repented of their sin.

Nineveh was the superpower of that day, much like Washington, Moscow, and Beijing are today, which suggests that the story of Jonah remains timely. God's character provides a model for us, both as individuals and as communities.

Jesus' Authority

Why is Jesus an authority on the image of God? Christ's death on the cross and resurrection accredit his link to God as the author of our faith (1 Cor 15:20–28; Heb 12:2). In fact, because the New Testament was written after Christ's death and resurrection, every sentence in the New Testament should be read as if prepended with the words: Because Christ rose from the dead, therefore…

The parables of Jesus should therefore be read as if penned by God himself, something worthy of further study. These five characteristics of God—mercy, grace, patience, love, and faithfulness—provide a powerful classification for Jesus' parables.

Context of Christian Spirituality

A complete spirituality addresses each of the four questions typically posed in philosophy:

1. Metaphysics—Who is God?

2. Anthropology—Who are we?

3. Epistemology—How do we know?

4. Ethics—What do we do about it? (Kreeft 2007, 6)

My first two books—*A Christian Guide to Spirituality* and *Life in Tension*—addressed the metaphysical question. My third book, *Called Along the Way*, explored the anthropological question in the first person. My fourth book, *Simple Faith*, examined the epistemological question. My fifth book, *Living in Christ*, centered on the ethics question. My sixth book, *Image and Illumination*, returned to Christian anthropology from a community perspective.

Image of God in the Parables builds on lessons learned in *Image and Illumination* with a renewed focus on metaphysics. It is written in a devotional format with a reflection, prayers, and questions for study. For those of you who may have wondered, I find the devotional format a compelling way to share my own meditations.

Soli Deo Gloria

∞

God of all Mercy,

All praise and honor, power and dominion, truth, and justice are yours because you created us in your image, male and female, and ransomed us through the life, death, and resurrection of Jesus Christ.

We confess that there is no law that we have not broken in spirit and in truth, nor have we loved you with all of our hearts and minds, nor have we loved our neighbor. We are shattered images undeserving of your love and attention.

Thank you for your love, both unconditional and conditional, loving us better than our own mothers and fathers, in spite of our rebellious nature and broken faith.

In the power of your Holy Spirit, break every chain with which Satan binds us, be it traumatic pain, impious griefs, blistering illnesses, or soul-crushing addictions. Come in our hearts and cleanse us of all such sin, transgressions, and iniquities that we might be whole again. Give us hearts and minds for you alone, and Christian friends and a faithful church to aid us in life's journey.

In Jesus' precious name, Amen.

Questions
1. What are three New Testament images of God?
2. What are several circumlocutions for the name of God?
3. What self-disclosure does God give to Moses?
4. What is interesting about the story of Jonah, other than the whale?

INTRODUCTION

The Face of God

What man of you, having a hundred sheep,
if he has lost one of them,
does not leave the ninety-nine in the open country,
and go after the one that is lost, until he finds it?
(Luke 15:4)

*T*he Lost Sheep (1898), a painting by Alfred Usher Soord (1868–1915), captured the enthusiasm of the great missionary movement of the late nineteenth century that followed the call by Dwight Moody to: "The evangelization of the world in this generation." (Longfield 1991, 18, 185). The painting pictures a shepherd hanging off a cliff to rescue a lost sheep stuck on a limb in imminent danger of either falling to its death or being eaten alive by a circling eagle.

This painting tells a story and draws us in. But what is that story? Even though we cannot see the face of the shepherd in Soord's painting, we immediately intuit that he is an honorable, trustworthy, and courageous man, someone devoted to his flock. Yet, we do not know his ethnicity, his religion, or even his age. Still, we want to emulate this shepherd as a role model.

For the believer, this painting evokes the image of an activist God who takes great risks to rescue sinners from impending death. We know this shepherd image from Psalm

23:1, which begins: "The Lord is my shepherd; I shall not want." Jesus himself called on this image in John 10:14: "I am the good shepherd. I know my own and my own know me." This image is poignant because we have more experience with bad shepherds than with good ones (Ezek 34).

Digging deeper into John 10, the story Jesus told may not be the one heard. Jesus heals a blind man during the feast of Tabernacles (John 7:1), while the shepherd discussion takes place during the feast of Dedication (John 10:22), which like Hanukkah commemorates the re-dedication of the temple by Judas Maccabees in 165 BC. The Maccabees led a rebellion against the Hellenization of Israel and the desecration of the temple by Antiochus Epiphanies—a very bad shepherd! While today John 10 is typically read along with Psalm 23 (good shepherds), the context suggests that Ezekiel 34 (bad shepherds) is the more apt sermon text.

For the unbeliever, bad shepherds like Antiochus Epiphanies would be a more common experience than good shepherds and would clearly not be hanging off cliffs for lost sheep. In preparing to paint, Soord clearly read Ezekiel 34:5–6: "My sheep were scattered; they wandered over all the mountains and on every high hill." Unbelievers almost certainly would not see the allegory so obvious to most believers.

This is not a painting that leaves the viewer without an emotional response. Even a materialist might recognize the magnetism of this art. A cynic might scoff at the idea of the shepherd's divine symbolism; a feminist might write off the story because the shepherd is male. A first-century Jerusalem resident might easily have seen the shepherd as a shady figure—a poor, smelly beggar or thief—not a Sunday school icon. A nonbeliever might reject the analogy obvious to believers as naive and work hard to come up with alternative narratives.

The point here is that Soord's painting, like the parable itself, forces the viewer to accept or reject the theme of the painting. Jesus himself says: "This is why I speak to them in parables, because seeing they do not see, and hearing they do not hear, nor do they understand." (Matt 13:13) The parable (and the painting) bring us into the presence of God and confront us with a decision of faith. Our hearts are either willing or not.

When Moses asked to see God's face, God cautioned him to look only at the tail of his robe as he passed by. God then said: "The Lord, the Lord, a God merciful and gracious, slow to anger, and abounding in steadfast love and faithfulness." (Exod 34:6) God's face in the Old Testament was veiled and elusive. Seeing only God's robe, Moses' face began to glow (Exod 34:29). It is only in the person of Jesus and through his parables that we get a fuller picture.

∞

Father God,

    All praise and honor, power and dominion, truth and justice are yours because you created us and have rescued us like a Good Shepherd in spite of our foolish wandering from your image and word.

    Forgive our wanton behavior, our directionless lives, and willful sinning when you have provided for all our needs, both physical and spiritual.

    Thank you for the life, death, and resurrection of Jesus, the teaching of his parables, and the guidance of the church, founded and provisioned by the Holy Spirit.

    Through the power of the Holy Spirit, draw us to yourself. Open our hearts, illumine our minds, and strengthen our hands in your service.

    In Jesus' precious name, Amen.

∞

Questions
1. What scriptural passages come to mind in the parable of the Lost Sheep?

2. What examples of bad shepherds can you name?
3. How does God describe himself to Moses?
4. What does it mean to have the glow?

Indirect Speech

> *For the kingdom of heaven is like a master of a house who went out early in the morning to hire laborers for his vineyard. After agreeing with the laborers for a denarius a day, he sent them into his vineyard.*
>
> (Matt 20:1–2)

In the early 1980s while I was in graduate school, a Russian friend invited me to a vodka party. My friend's Russian, ex-pat friends affectionally referred to him as Boris the spy because of his strong family ties to the KGB. At this party, an inebriated Russian friend of his, a professor, came up to me and began translating an article from *Pravda*, the official newspaper of the Communist Party of the USSR.

He started by asking: How could Pravada be so openly critical of the government? The article read: How could the government of Beethoven, Brahms, and Goethe so openly lie about the murder of so many innocent civilians in concentration camps by Adolf Hitler? The professor immediately substituted: How could the government of Tchaikovsky, Rimsky Korsakov, and Dostoevsky openly lie about the murder of so many innocent civilians in Ukraine by Comrade Stalin? He said that for Russians used to lies and doublespeak, the allegorical implications of this article were as transparent as they were astounding.

Under the threat of death for offering comments critical of the power structure of his day (e.g. Mark 6:27), Jesus spoke in parables. Indirect speech—circumlocution, similes, metaphors, poetry, proverbs, and allegory—are common genres in the New Testament. The most extreme form of indirect speech is seen in the apocalyptic literature of the Book of Revelation. It is no secret why the countries with the most repressive governments often generate the best poetry—indirect speech is the language of repressed people.

Circumlocutions

As already mentioned in the preface, the Bible uses numerous circumlocutions—indirect references—for God's name. A parable is an elegant form of circumlocution that Jesus began using after the Pharisees began to plot against him (Matt 12–13).

New Testament references to the Kingdom of God (Mark, Luke) or the Kingdom of Heaven (Matthew) sound like modern media reports citing informed sources at the White House. Everyone assumes that directly or indirectly such references come from the President. Almost all of Jesus' parables refer to God, while rabbinic parables typically elucidate a passage of scripture (Blomberg 2012, 77). Jesus' parables are unique in their focus on God.

Allegory

Allegory can be thought of as a narrative pattern where the context has been switched. In the parable of the vineyard, a landowner recruits workers at different times during the day of the harvest but pays them all the same wage. For any business, this would be odd. Here, a vineyard or garden is a frequent metaphor for the nation of Israel and the landowner in the parable is a reference to God, which is obvious because of the circumlocution: "For the kingdom of heaven is like." (Matt 20:1) The hard part in interpreting the parable is to see that the denarius, a Roman coin, is a symbol of salvation or eternal life (Kissenger 1979, 2–3).

Interpreting the denarius as a symbol of eternal life gives spiritual meaning to the parable. As a unit of monetary value, the denarius makes the landowner out to be extremely generous, but the missional interpretation of the parable is hidden. Thus, a believer is likely to understand the inference immediately, while a nonbeliever might only engage in a bit of head scratching. For the believer, the gift of eternal life is something of infinite value that is not easily divided, not something likely to evoke jealousy on the part of laborers hired early in the day as described in the story. This caveat suggests a limit on the allegory, even though the primary message is clear.

∞

Lord of the Sabbath,

All praise and honor, power and dominion, truth and justice are yours, because you speak to us plainly in the language of faith, veiled to those unable to believe.

Forgive us when we refuse to listen, close our eyes, and pay no attention to fragrance of the Holy Spirit in our lives.

Thank you for deliverance from the evil around us, for the guidance of your image, and the healing that comes from accepting your grace.

In the power of the Holy Spirit, draw us closer to yourself. Open our hearts, illumine our minds, and strength our hands in your service, now and always.

In the name of Father, the Son, and the Holy Spirit, Amen.

∞

Question
1. Why do repressed people use indirect speech?
2. What are some examples of indirect speech found in the

New Testament.
3. What is a circumlocution?
4. What is allegory?

Parable as Genre

Nathan said to David, You are the man!
(2 Sam 12:7)

In 2 Samuel 12:1–7, the prophet Nathan tells King David the story of two men, one rich and the other poor. The poor man has only one small lamb that the rich man steals and slaughters to serve his guest. When David hears this story, he becomes indignant because he had been a shepherd and understood the cruelty of the rich man. When Nathan declares that he is this man, because of David's sin with Bathsheba, David is cut to the core and repents of his sin. This parable of the lamb is an allegory, where the context is shifted and the true context is only revealed at the end of the story. The true context then becomes the key, like the denarius in the parable of the vineyard, to the entire story.

Although the story of Nathan's parable told to David is normally held up as the only example of a parable in the Old Testament to compare with Jesus' parables, the story is not described in the text as a parable. When the Old Testament uses the word, parable, it is in the context of stories of divine judgment.

Old Testament Parables

Our use of the word *parable* is transliterated from the

Greek word *parabole* that is used only three times in the Old Testament (Ps 78:2, Ezek 17:2; 24:3). In each case, the parable given is a prophecy of judgment on the nation of Israel for their lack of faith.

Psalm 78 recounts the history of Israel during the desert wandering following the Exodus from Egypt and the unwillingness of even Moses to rely on God provision, when he struck rather than spoke to the rock at Kadesh, as God directed:

> Because you did not believe in me, to uphold me as holy in the eyes of the people of Israel, therefore you shall not bring this assembly into the land that I have given them. (Num 20:12)

The judgment against Moses is personal. The parable in this case is the story of Israel's disobedience.

With a story about two eagles, Ezekiel 17 recounts Israel's attempt to rebel against Babylon by forming an alliance with Pharaoh in Egypt rather than relying on God. Ezekiel 24 talks about Babylon's siege against Jerusalem and the destruction to come as being like a pot boiling a meat stew.

Parable Defined

The word for parable in the Greek is *parabole* that has two definitions:

1. Something that serves as a model or example pointing

beyond itself for later realization, type, figure, or

2. A narrative or saying of varying length, designed to illustrate a truth especially through comparison or simile, contrast, illustration, parable, proverb, maxim (BDAG 5556).

The Greek definition is close to our common understanding of a parable from those given by Jesus.

The Hebrew word translated as *parabole* in the Greek is *mashal*. *Mashal* carries these inferences:

1. A proverbial saying, brief terse sentence of popular sagacity,
2. A prophetic figurative discourse,
3. A by-word,
4. A similitude, parable,
5. A poem of various kinds,
6. A sentence of ethical wisdom (BDB 5753).

This is a wide range of meanings for *mashal* in the Hebrew, inclusive of our understanding of Jesus' parables, but also inclusive of Solomon's many proverbs and things that we do not normally think of as parables.

Genre and Character

Jesus extended the genre of parables to reflect the character of God.

Our excursion into Greek and Hebrew suggests that the focus of Jesus's parables on God extended the Old Testament parable normally associated with divine judgment to offer a fuller characterization of God. The God of the Old Testament describes himself to Moses as merciful, gracious, patient, loving, and faithful (Exod 34:6). The characterization of God as wrathful is limited to situations where the people of Israel have been disobedient to their covenantal obligations or display hardness of heart like Pharaoh (Exod 4:21). God is not capricious like many other deities in the ancient world.

This observation leads Matthew Elliot (2009, 46–47) to articulate a cognitive theory of emotions. Like God of the Old Testament, we get angry about things that are important to us. Elliott (2009, 53–54) writes: "If the cognitive theory is correct, emotions become an integral part of our reason and our ethics," informing and reinforcing moral behavior.

Jesus extended the Old Testament treatment of parables in two ways. First, while divine judgment in the Old Testament is primarily corporal (the nation of Israel), Jesus' judgment is more personal, relating to individual demonstrations of faith or disobedience (e.g. Matt 25) as in the example of Moses at Kadesh. Second, Jesus associates parables with attributes of God beyond judgment—mercy, grace, patience, love, and faithfulness (Exod 34:6). Thus, God becomes our father not only in the Lord's prayer, but also in being pictured as a God who displays a range of attributes and associated emotions. We might say that Jesus pictured God the Father as more human, but that characterization neglects the fuller testimony of the Old Testament—he always was more than just a wrathful God.

∞

Father God,

All praise and honor, power and dominion, truth and justice are yours because you reveal to us in Jesus a more nuanced picture of yourself, someone we can trust and emulate.

Forgive us for not remembering the discipline of our youth when we tried your patience and did not display your mercy, grace, patience, love, or truthfulness.

Thankfully, you are more patient and merciful than we are.

In the power of your Holy Spirit, grant us your strength of character in dealing graciously with one another.

In Jesus' precious name, Amen.

∞

Questions
1. What is the focus of Old Testament parables?
2. How does Jesus extend the Old Testament notion of a parable?
3. What is the cognitive theory of emotions?
4. What is wrong with characterizing the Old Testament notion of a wrathful God?

Parables in a Postmodern Context

> *The fear of the LORD is the beginning of knowledge;*
> *fools despise wisdom and instruction.*
> (Prov 1:7)

We know from philosophy that the existence of God can neither be logically proven or disproven, much like the existence of an objective truth. Placher (1989, 34) writes citing Wittgenstein:

> When we find the foundations, it turns out they are being held up by the rest of the house. If theologians try to defend their claims by starting with basic, foundational truths that any rational person would have to believe or observations independent of theory and assumptions, they are trying to do something that our best philosophers tell us is impossible.

In plain English, the argument here is that our empirical observations (the grass is green) cannot be separated from our initial definitions (green is the color of a tomato leaf).

Because enlightenment scholars have failed to find a logistically defensible basis for faith, Christian philosopher Alan Plantinga (2000, xi) proposed the concept of warranted faith. If we engage in a decision for faith when our mental capacities are functioning correctly, then that decision cannot be challenged as philosophically deficient in the manner in which Marx, Freud, and Nietsche slandered the faith in God (Plantinga 2000, 136–

142).

Evidence of God's Work in the World

The Bible talks extensively about truth. Jesus describes the Holy Spirit as the Spirit of Truth (John 14:17), and Peter calls the Gospel the Way of Truth (2 Pet 2:2). The Apostle Paul writes that: "Those who would worship the creation rather than the creator have 'exchanged the truth about God for a lie.'" (Rom 1:25; Howard 2018, 178) Furthermore, John testifies as an eyewitness to the truth of the Gospel (1 John 1:1–3). Later, we read:

> We are from God. Whoever knows God listens to us; whoever is not from God does not listen to us. By this we know the Spirit of truth and the spirit of error. Beloved, let us love one another, for love is from God, and whoever loves has been born of God and knows God. Anyone who does not love does not know God, because God is love. (1 John 4:6–8)

Here, the Apostle John sees love as evidence of God's existence and revelation to us.

Because of the many false definitions of love floating around in the postmodern world, John's focus on love is less helpful than in previous eras. Still, John does two interesting things in this passage. First, John assumes that the presence of God can be observed in people. This implies that, although proof of God's existence cannot be logically proved, we still have evidence. Second, this evidence of God's existence is relational. Love requires an object; it does not stand alone.

The criterion for faith then becomes: Is the Christian story about God more credible than alternative stories about how the world works? Hart (2009, ix) writes: "It may be impossible to provide perfectly irrefutable evidence for one's conclusions, but it is certainly possible to amass evidence sufficient to confirm them beyond plausible doubt." The criteria for faith is nothing more than a simplified version of the scientific method.

The Role of the Parables

In the postmodern context in which logical arguments about God's existence are insufficient, Jesus' parables present descriptions about how God works in our everyday world. In a first-century worldview, the transcendence of God was not disputed, but God's character and his concern for everyday people was poorly understood. In the postmodern world, this description is reversed. God's character and concern are at least superficially assumed, but his transcendence is questioned. If his transcendence cannot be demonstrated, then our knowledge about his character and concern appears tenuous.

The argument from the parables is that God's transcendence is inferred from the relational credibility of his character and concern for everyday people. This is an argument from the lesser to the greater, an *a fortiori* argument. God's love is like that of a father for his two sons, only greater, as in the parable of the Prodigal Son (Luke 15:11–32). We know how much parents love their children; the parable relates that love to the love of God for his people. Relationally, this argument is immediately obvious.

In our cynical age, we tire of hearing endless, unresolved stories of disobedient children and abusive parents. Stories of joy and healing are good news to our sorry ears. Jesus' parables are like the water offered to the desert traveler lost, faint-hearted, and close to death.

∞

Blessed Lord Jesus,

All praise and honor, power and dominion, truth and justice are yours because you came to us and spoke in our language, the language of daily life.

Forgive us when we talk in circles, trying to impress our friends with arguments that we don't understand fully ourselves.

Thank you for your patience, your willingness to listen to us, and reason with us so that we understand.

In the power of your Holy Spirit, remain with us, guide

us, and provision us with your many blessings, like a caring father. Support our families, heal our diseases, and be especially present in our afflictions.

In Jesus' precious name, Amen.

∞

Questions
1. Can God's existence be logically proven?
2. What is warranted faith?
3. How does the Apostle John argue for God's existence?
4. What is an *a fortiori* argument?

MERCY

The Good Samaritan

Be merciful, even as your Father is merciful.
(Luke 6:36)

The first characteristic of God in Exodus 34:6 is mercy. The Hebrew word for mercy *rahum* (BDB 9028) is used in conjunction with *hannun* (BDB 3259), both of which rhyme and translate as compassion, suggesting a compound idiom or hendiadys. The same problem exists in the Septuagint Greek words, *oiktirmon* and *elemon*. In English, a judicial distinction is often given where mercy is not getting a punishment that one deserves, while compassion is receiving a blessing that one did not earn (Finney 1999,143).

This translation problem continues in the New Testament. Consider: "For he says to Moses, I will have mercy on whom I have mercy, and I will have compassion on whom I have compassion." (Rom 9:15) The Apostle Paul uses both Greek words in this sentence, which are translated into the English as both mercy and compassion. Jacob benefits from God's favor while his brother Essau does not, an example of divine sovereignty (Rom 9:13; 9:18). A sovereign action is possible because the benefit is not earned and no obligation is implied. We scratch our heads on reading this story because we cringe at the idea that God favors one sinner over another. Some of the most intractable family controversies arise in negotiating whose sins are forgivable and whose not.

Interestingly, the Hebrew word for mercy is only used to describe God, making it difficult to offer a parable describing God's characteristic within a human context.

The Good Samaritan

The legal context of the parable of the Good Samaritan sheds light on the distinction between mercy and compassion. When the Samaritan finds the man stripped and beaten by robbers, the text reads: "But a Samaritan, as he journeyed, came to where he was, and when he saw him, he had compassion." (Luke 10:33) The Greek word for compassion is *esplagnisthe*, which is unrelated to either mercy or compassion in the Hebrew cited above, but means something like: His heart (guts) went out for him.

Later, when the Jewish lawyer talking to Jesus recapitulates the sentiment of the parable, he uses the word *eleos* (Luke 10:37), that is translated into English as mercy. While *eleos* can also be translated as compassion, as in Exodus 34:6, the lawyer clearly has no compassion for the man robbed and, perhaps, wonders whether he deserved the beating he received. Being forgiven of the offense of being a Samaritan (a Jewish prejudice) is accordingly described not as compassion, but as mercy. Thus, the storyteller emphases the emotional distance traveled here by choosing to start with an entirely different word for compassion (*esplagnisthe*).

In the parable, Jesus uses a lawyer's trick to make a similar point. The lawyer begins this discussion asking who is my neighbor? (Luke 10:29) The word neighbor is a noun and the lawyer asks the question so as to restrict his obligation under the law. Jesus converts the noun (a neighbor) into a verb (to be a neighbor), asking: "Which of these three, do you think, proved to be a neighbor to the man who fell among the robbers?" (Luke 10:36) In doing this, Jesus converts a limited obligation into one that is potentially limitless. Thus, the emotional distance traveled implied by the word choice above is paralleled by the legal distance traveled implied by the noun-to-verb transformation.

Contending Contexts

In the early church, parables were often interpreted allegorically. With Adolf Jülicher (1857–1938), the focus in interpretation shifted away from allegory. Jülicher believed that parables were "literal speech and self-explanatory" (Kissenger 1979, 76). He offered a classification of four types of parables: the simile, the similitude, the fable, and the example story (Kissenger

1979, 72–73). This change in emphasis opened up parables to modern forms of criticism, such as the form criticism: "Rudolf Bultmann notes that every literary category has its own *Sitz im Leben* (life situation), whether it be worship in its different forms, or work, or hunting, or war." (Kissenger 1979, 102)

More recent scholarship has focused on the historical context of the parables, of which two are important: Jesus' context and the context of the early church. For someone living in a hostile environment, public statements must necessarily be veiled in poetic or symbolic language. We see this problem today in political speech where like-minded members of a particular party will speak openly of controversial topics in coded language, poorly understood by outsiders.

Jesus' context differed from the context of the early church suggesting that he might make allegorical statements whose meaning was lost or deemed less important only a few years later. A modern example might be the allegories found in the Wizard of Oz (1937) film, like the "follow the yellow-brick road" song that referred to a recently abandoned Gold Standard (1931). Today the song is cute, but not obviously a political statement.

Parable's *Sitz in Leben*

Mercy is a fitting focus of the story of the Good Samaritan because Jews hated Samaritans. The Samaritan had to overcome prejudice (show mercy) in order to show love to the man left for dead. In the same way, we experience God's love through his mercy in sending Christ to die for our sins on the cross.

James concludes much the same from God's attributes when he observes: "For judgment is without mercy to one who has shown no mercy. Mercy triumphs over judgment." (Jas 2:13) Here James has restated Jesus' Beatitude in the negative—it is a curse to be judged without mercy (see Matt 5:7). Judgment requires truth, which—like love—follows mercy on the list of God's attributes in Exodus 34:6.

The link between judgment and mercy points us back to the atoning work of Christ, as the Apostle Peter observed:

> Blessed be the God and Father of our Lord Jesus Christ! According to his great mercy, he has caused us to be born again to a living hope through the resurrection of Jesus Christ from the dead, to an inheritance that is imperishable, undefiled, and unfading, kept in heaven for you, who by God's power are being guarded through faith for a salvation ready to be revealed in the last time. (1 Pet 1:3–5)

The path to salvation through Christ (and his love) is by way of his mercy.

∞

Beloved Savior,

All glory and honor, power and dominion, truth and justice are yours because you speak to us in our pain and offer us comfort in our afflictions.

Forgive us for bringing pain and afflictions on ourselves through foolishness, laziness, and boredom.

Thank for your presence in our hour of need, loneliness, and clouded thinking.

In the power of your Holy Spirit, build our families, churches, and communities according to your plan for our lives that we might sparkle in the midst of darkness and despair.

In Jesus' precious name, Amen.

∞

Questions
1. How do you distinguish mercy and grace? What does the Bible say?
2. What is your chief take-away from the parable of the Good Samaritan?
3. What two important contexts do Jesus' parables have in the New Testament?
4. How do you define Sitz in Leben?

The Unforgiving Servant

> *For if you forgive others their trespasses,*
> *your heavenly Father will also forgive you,*
> *but if you do not forgive others their trespasses,*
> *neither will your Father forgive your trespasses.*
> (Matt 6:14–15)

Following the judicial distinction between mercy and compassion, mercy denotes social and emotional separation while compassion connotes greater social and emotional affinity. Both speak to God's attributes but the pride of place in the pantheon of attributes goes to mercy because before Christ's sacrifice on the cross, original sin separated us from God.

Judicial mercy draws our attention to God the Father's transcendence and giving of Mosaic law while judicial compassion draws us to Christ's humanity, God's immanence. As the Apostle Paul observed:

> For one will scarcely die for a righteous person—though perhaps for a good person one would dare even to die—but God shows his love for us in that while we were still sinners, Christ died for us. (Rom 5:7–8)

For this reason, perhaps, mercy is among the Beatitudes mentioned in Jesus' Sermon on the Mount in Matthew 5, while love is not. Mercy is more primal even if it is motivated by love.

The Unforgiving Servant

The mercy of God is clearly displayed in the parable of the Unforgiving Servant, where we read:

> Therefore the kingdom of heaven may be compared to a king who wished to settle accounts with his servants. When he began to settle, one was brought to him who owed him ten thousand talents. And since he could not pay, his master ordered him to be sold, with his wife and children and all that he had, and payment to be made. So the servant fell on his knees, imploring him, have patience with me, and I will pay you everything. And out of pity for him, the master of that servant released him and forgave him the debt. (Matt 18:23–27).

Here we see a soft-hearted king who forgives an enormous debt out of pity for the debtor and his family. The enormity of the debt suggests a king forgiving the debt of a regional governor—the slave sale would, by contrast, be merely a punitive, symbolic gesture. The opening phrase references the kingdom of heaven, a classic circumlocution for God. The overwhelming sum of money forgiven is a second tell because of God's overwhelming generosity throughout scripture, but especially seen in the Gospel of John (e.g. 2:6–10; 6:5–14; 21:4–13).

The parable, however, has an unexpected twist.

The servant, having been forgiven an enormous sum, turns on a fellow servant who owes him a tiny sum and treats him harshly (Matt 28:28–30). When the king learned what his servant had done, he became angry, summoned him, and threw him into jail (Matt 18:31–35). Thus, we learn that it is not enough to know that God is merciful—we are to model God's mercy to others.

Echoes of Creation

The need to model God's behavior to others is hardwired into our creation, as we read: "So God created man in his own image, in the image of God he created him; male and female he created them." (Gen 1:27) Being created in the image of God, we are expected to mirror not so much God's appearance, but his ethical teaching. After creating the heaven and the earth, God created light that he immediately declares to be good (Gen 1:3–4). The point here is that the parable is making explicit a principle that the Bible has reiterated from the beginning.

Lest we overlook an important point, note that God gets angry when we neglect to reflect his divine image. In the parable, the king gets angry at the servant he forgave who refused to practice forgiveness and the king re-institutes the penalty for nonpayment of the servant's debt. God's wrath reinforces his own teaching and is neither arbitrary nor capricious. God really wants us to practice mercy.

The Law and the Prophets

The Apostle Paul, like a good Rabbi, often looked to principles taught in the Books of the Law (the first five books of the Old Testament) to be applied or explained in the Prophets (all the other Old Testament books). God's mercy is, for example, a theme in the Book of Jonah.

God told Jonah: "Arise, go to Nineveh, that great city, and call out against it, for their evil has come up before me." (Jonah 1:2) Jonah hated the Ninevites because Nineveh was the hometown of Sennacherib, King of Assyria, who had seized all of Judea, except for Jerusalem (Isa 36:1). Jonah fled by boat from God to avoid preaching to the Ninevites, was thrown overboard in a storm, and was rescued by a whale. God then asked him again to go to Nineveh. Jonah went, he preached to the Ninevites, and they repented of their sin. God forgave them and spared the city, much to Jonah's consternation. (Jonah 3:10, 4:1)

When asked why he attempted to run away from God, Jonah cited God's mercy (Jonah 4:2). Jonah wanted Nineveh destroyed, not forgiven.

God's merciful character is consistent across Holy Scripture. In Exodus 34:6, we learn that God is merciful, in Jonah 3:10 we see God offering mercy to Nineveh, and in Matthew

18:27 we are reminded that God practices mercy. Even post resurrection after his disciples deserted him, Jesus treated them mercifully—a point of special interest to us today.

This consistency has led theologians to describe God's character as immutable. If God's character somehow changed over time or that God learned through experience, then we might worry that he also would forget his promises.

∞

God of All Mercy,

All praise and honor, power and dominion, truth and justice are yours, because you forgive our sins when we repent of them and remember your promises.

Forgive us of our inconsistent emotions and behaviors that lead us to sin and to neglect our promises.

Thank you for the gift of forgiveness granted to us because of Jesus' death on the cross.

In the power of your Holy Spirit, draw us closer to you day by day that we might draw strength from your strength, grace from your grace, and peace from your peace.

In Jesus' precious name, Amen.

∞

Questions
1. Why does mercy have pride of place in the pantheon of

God's attributes?
2. What does the parable of the Unforgiving Servant teach us about God's mercy?
3. What do we learn from the parable about God's wrath?
4. What does it mean to be created in the image of God?

The Barren Fig Tree

> *For no good tree bears bad fruit,*
> *nor again does a bad tree bear good fruit,*
> *for each tree is known by its own fruit.*
> (Luke 6:43–44)

Jesus talked frequently about fruit as a mark of identity. Just as a tree is known for its fruit, the heart is known by its actions. He said: "Thus you will recognize them by their fruits." (Matt. 7:20) Believers and prophets alike are to be measured by their fruits. John the Baptist was even more direct, measuring repentance by the actions that followed—presumably penance—in the context of divine judgment (Matt 3:8).

The Apostle Paul also talked about fruit: "But the fruit of the Spirit is love, joy, peace, patience, kindness, goodness, faithfulness, gentleness, self-control; against such things there is no law." (Gal 5:22–23) He contrasted the fruit of the spirit with the desires of the flesh and the works that follow:

> Now the works of the flesh are evident: sexual immorality, impurity, sensuality, idolatry, sorcery, enmity, strife, jealousy, fits of anger, rivalries, dissensions, divisions, envy, drunkenness, orgies, and things like these. (Gal 5:19–21)

The controlling idea here is that the desires of the heart are revealed in the actions of the body. The Apostle James underscored this same relationship and tied it to the patience of a farmer who had to wait after planting seed for the rains to come and the plants to grow (Jas 5:7).

Parable of the Barren Fig Tree

Jesus told this parable:

> A man had a fig tree planted in his vineyard, and he came seeking fruit on it and found none. And he said to the vinedresser, Look, for three years now I have come seeking fruit on this fig tree, and I find none. Cut it down. Why should it use up the ground? And he answered him, Sir, let it alone this year also, until I dig around it and put on manure. Then if it should bear fruit next year, well and good; but if not, you can cut it down. (Luke 13:6–9)

Notice the three actors in this parable: a landowner, a vinedresser, and a fig tree. Allegorically, the conversation here is a discussion between God the Father (the landowner) and Jesus Christ (the vinedresser) about a certain person (the fig tree). Here the vinedresser is arguing for more time for the fig tree to yield fruit and offering to weed and fertilize the tree. The tree has no inherent value other than to yield fruit and it is not currently yielding fruit.

The landowner offers mercy to the fig tree in the form of additional growing time, but this mercy has limits—only one more year to grow. Like the parable of the unforgiving servant, the mercy offered is limited—the servant forgiven was expected to offer similar mercy to his own debtors, a kind of fruit of repentance that John the Baptist required (Matt 3:8).

Mercy as a Divine Attribute

As described above, mercy serves as a test of those receiving it with the implication that judgment will follow for those who fail the test. God's mercy is not carte blanc: It describes who he is, but it also comes in the context of obligations and limits on our own behavior.

In law, we find two kinds of justice: Criminal justice and restorative justice. Criminal justice serves to punish offenders and leaves it up to them to abide by the law in the future by weighing the costs (suffering penalties under law) and benefits (avoiding future penalties) of noncompliance. Restorative justice focuses on reforming the offender. Typically, juveniles face restorative justice, while adults face criminal justice.

The Bible presents God as generally offering restorative justice. The story of Cain and Abel is an example of this restorative justice. When Cain gets angry with his brother, Abel, God advises him to deal with his anger (Gen 4:6–7). When Cain then kills Abel, God curses him to be a wanderer (Gen 4:12). When Cain complains that he cannot bear his punishment, God protects him from the revenge of other men by placing a mark on him (Gen 4:15). Had God imposed the penalty of death on Cain, it would have been criminal justice (Gen 9:6). As it was, Cain received restorative justice, even though we never hear that he actually reformed.

In the parable of the Barren Fig Tree, I have always wondered how many years the vinedresser didn't argue with the landowner for the fig tree. In our backyard, we have a barren persimmon tree. I have for years argued to cut it down and for years my wife has told me: Give it one more year. Knowing the heart of God, I expect that a similar outcome would follow.

∞

Almighty Father,

All praise and honor, power and dominion, truth and justice are yours, because you taught us the meaning of mercy and practiced forgiveness before we had any idea of either.

We confess that we are slow learners, especially when it requires us to forgive others. Forgive our hardened hearts, clouded minds, and lazy hands that never seem to get it right.

Thank you for the sacrifice of Jesus of Nazareth on the cross. Teach us to emulate his sacrifice for those around us.

In the power of your Holy Spirit, grant us strength to endure sacrifice, grace to share with others, and the peace that passes all understanding.

In Jesus' precious name, Amen.

∞

Questions
1. What role does fruit play in understanding the hearts of others?
2. What happened in the parable of the Barren Fig Tree?
3. What are two kinds of justice?
4. What kind of justice does the Bible associate with God?

The Tax Collector and the Pharisee

> *In the course of time Cain brought to the LORD*
> *an offering of the fruit of the ground,*
> *and Abel also brought of the firstborn of his flock*
> *and of their fat portions.*
> *And the LORD had regard for Abel and his offering,*
> *but for Cain and his offering he had no regard.*
> (Gen 4:3–5)

Evangelist Charles Finney (1792–1875), sometimes called the father of revivalism, was trained as a lawyer and was known to preach fire and brimstone (Galli and Olsen 2000, 67). He intuitively understood the judicial context of mercy and the critical role played by original sin. He wrote:

> The guilty man, if he desires to have mercy from the executive, must admit the rightness of the law and of the penalty. Otherwise, he arrays himself against the law and cannot be trusted in the community. (Finney 1999, 151)

For the accused, pleading guilty satisfies the judicial requirement for mercy because pleading not guilty denies that a law has been broken. Pleading guilty also relieves the prosecutor of the burden of proving guilt and a lengthy trial, which reduces public expense—an enormous concern of prosecutors.

Original sin is the doctrine that argues that, although we were created sinless, sin entered the human race when Adam and Eve ate the forbidden fruit (Gen 3:6). This is collective sin where the sin of the fathers is passed onto the children (Exod 34:7). The cycle of collective sin and guilt was broken when a sinless Christ died on the cross, paying the penalty of sin for us all. Atonement for collective sin, an event foretold by the Prophet Jeremiah (31:29–30), could only be made with a divine sacrifice.

The argument that we are all basically good (that is, are not guilty of original sin) negates the principal work of Christ, who is argued throughout the New Testament to have died for our sins (e.g. 1 Cor 15:3). No sin; no need of salvation. It also implies that Christ is not divine because Christ could not have been a sinless sacrifice for us all unless he were also God.

Consequently, God's attribute of being merciful stands as a critical argument in understanding central tenants of the Christian faith. As an attorney and evangelist, Finney played a key role in raising the common understanding of our Christian faith as well as helping found the Evangelical movement in the nineteenth century.

Lest anyone argue that the judicial understanding of mercy was a nineteenth century innovation, remember that law played a larger role in Judaism, which provided the backdrop for the New Testament. New Testament writers wrote about Gospel in a cultural context where legal arguments dominated everyday life.

The Pharisee and the Tax Collector

The manner in which Jesus distinguished pleas of guilty versus not guilty play a key role in this parable about prayer:

> Two men went up into the temple to pray, one a Pharisee and the other a tax collector. The Pharisee, standing by himself, prayed thus: God, I thank you that I am not like other men, extortioners, unjust, adulterers, or even like this tax collector. I fast twice a week; I give tithes of all that I get. But the tax collector, standing far off, would not even lift up his eyes to heaven, but beat his breast, saying, God, be merciful to me, a sinner! I tell you, this man went down to his house justified, rather than the other. For everyone who exalts himself will be humbled, but the one who humbles himself will be exalted. (Luke 18:9–14)

In this story, the Pharisee clearly believes that he is not guilty (pleads innocent) of having transgressed Mosaic law, while the Tax Collector sees himself as guilty (pleads guilty). Here God plays the role of a judge who renders a verdict of justified to the Tax Collector, but not to the Pharisee. Implicit in this story is the concept of original sin (Ps 14) because both men are judged, which was culturally unexpected.

This parable focuses on the word *dikaio* (BDAG 2005), which translates as justified. The two primary definitions have a legal context, meaning: 1. to take up a legal cause, show justice, do justice, take up a cause; or 2. to render a favorable verdict, vindicate. While the judge in this parable renders the verdict, no penalty is mentioned.

Cain and Abel

The absence of a penalty is interesting because this parable focuses on two devout men in the temple, which excludes secular people not in the temple whose penalty for non-worship would be culturally more obvious. These types of men are explicit archetypes where one is proud and the other humble. We might compare these two men with Cain and his brother Abel, who presented their gifts to God before the altar. Cain's gift is rejected, while Abel's is accepted by God in his unexplained, sovereign decision.

In another context, we might describe this parable as taking the form of a parody or analogy (Dikkers 2018, 96–104). Because Jesus spoke in person, we might envision his expressions or pantomime as he told this story. Even today, rabbis can be hilarious speakers. Casting two devout men in the context of worship, one accepted and the other rejected, might be taken as a first-century, literary trope, perhaps embarrassing for Pharisees and humorous to others.

Noting a humorous context humanizes Jesus and reinforces the focus on attitude that is given in the parable's introduction.

∞

Blessed Lord Jesus,

All power and dominion, glory and honor, truth and justice are yours, because you speak to us with stories that we cannot help but repeat to display God's nature.

Forgive us when we fail to get it or refuse to acknowledge what our hearts and minds tell us is obviously true.

Thank you for your patience with us, offering us mercy rather than justice when we clearly do not deserve mercy and cannot stand in the face of true justice.

In the power of your Holy Spirit, give us open hearts, teachable minds, and helping hands that we might grow more like Jesus every day.

In Jesus' precious name, Amen.

∞

Questions
1. Who was Charles Finney? Why should we care?
2. How do court pleas inform our understanding of mercy?
3. What story does the Parable of the Pharisee and the Tax Collector mimic?
4. Do you think that God has a sense of humor?

Applying Mercy

> *Blessed are the merciful, for they shall receive mercy.*
> (Matt 5:7)

In the parables examined in this chapter, we begin to see the nature of God's mercy.

In the Good Samaritan, we learn that mercy requires a visceral reaction: Our hearts lean into mercy more than our heads. God is emotionally involved in our lives and our salvation. Furthermore, God's forgiveness overcomes all prejudice.

In the Unforgiving Servant, we see that God is willing to forgive those who repent of their sin and ask for his forgiveness. The only unforgivable sin is the refusal to believe. Still, our forgiveness comes with the obligation to extend mercy to those who sin against us.

In the Barren Fig Tree, we hear about the limits on God's patience. God's mercy does not mean that we can ignore him forever, like the man who plans to express belief on his deathbed. What happens if death comes too quickly for a confession? Furthermore, because a tree is known for its fruit, God is well aware that good fruit in a person comes from a good heart, which needs to be cultivated. Much as anything, the Barren Fig Tree is a parable about Christian formation.

In the Pharisee and the Tax Collector, we find a sovereign

God who favors humble believers. Humility before God clearly trumps simple worship, because both the Pharisee and the tax collector are presumably devout men offering prayer in the temple.

Stepping away from the parables for a minute, how does the Bible more generally teach that we should express mercy?

Sodom and Gomorrah

The story of the destruction of Sodom and Gomorrah is often interpreted primarily in terms of the judgment of God on these two cities for their sexual sin, including homosexual sin. Yet the context of the story is a dialogue between God and Abraham that begins with:

> The LORD said, Shall I hide from Abraham what I am about to do, seeing that Abraham shall surely become a great and mighty nation, and all the nations of the earth shall be blessed in him? (Gen 18:17–18)

While the judgment of the cities is topical, the story focuses on Abraham's handling of God's disclosure. What does Abraham do? Abraham immediately intercedes for Sodom and Gomorrah, expressing mercy for the people of Sodom and Gomorrah in prayer.

The key phrase in Abraham's intercession is: "Will you [God] indeed sweep away the righteous with the wicked?" (Gen

18:23) God does not spare the cities, but he expresses mercy to Abraham by sending his angel to rescue Abraham's nephew Lot and his family.

In this passage, God reveals his judgment to Abraham, a stand in for the rest of us, to see how Abraham will react. In this example, Abraham passes the test when he exhibits compassion for the cities and engages God in intercessory prayer.

The Reluctant Prophet

How many of us would pass God's test of Abraham? In scripture, the counter-example to Abraham arises in the story of the Prophet Jonah. In this short story, we read:

> Now the word of the LORD came to Jonah the son of Amittai, saying, Arise, go to Nineveh, that great city, and call out against it, for their evil has come up before me. (Jonah 1:1–2)

God's disclosure to Jonah is similar to that of Abraham. Nineveh is another evil city that God told his prophet he would destroy. But unlike Sodom and Gomorrah, God offers the city mercy by sending Jonah to "call out against it."

Nineveh was the hometown of Sennacherib king of Assyria, who had seized all of Judea, except for Jerusalem (Isa 36:1). Jonah hated the Ninevites and, instead of going to preach God's mercy to them, he got on a ship to escape from God and his mission. Then, as every Sunday school kid knows, a storm came up, the sailors tossed Jonah overboard, and he is swallowed by a whale that, after three days, spits him up on a beach. God then repeats his request for Jonah to go to Nineveh.

In this response, Jonah recites Exodus 34:6, which recounts God's character traits. Knowing God is merciful, Jonah refused to preach repentance to the Ninevites, but later does so reluctantly and they do repent, averting God's wrath, much to Jonah's consternation (Jonah 3:10, 4:1).

Judgment and Mercy in the End Times

Knowing that we are blessed to be a blessing and that God shares his plans for judgment with us through scripture and revelation, our attitude about those under judgment should change. Judgment of those outside the community of faith comes as a test of the hearts for those inside the community. Think about John's prophecy about the end times:

> The nations raged, but your wrath came, and the time for the dead to be judged, and for rewarding your servants, the prophets and saints, and those who fear your name, both small and great, and for destroying the destroyers of the earth. (Rev 11:18)

Do we cheer the destruction of sinners, like Jonah, or intercede in prayer, like Abraham? Scripture clearly shows that God's heart runs to mercy quicker than ours, which may explain why the New Testament places a high priority on evangelism.

∞

Almighty God,

All praise and honor, power and dominion, truth and justice are yours, because you offer mercy to sinners without prejudice and model mercy to us in our weaknesses and shame.

We confess that we are never so merciful as you, though we have been the recipients of your mercy since Jesus died on the cross to pay our penalty for sin.

Thank you for the gift of life, health, family, and all manner of blessings. Help us to remain thankful and to share your good news with those around us.

In the power of your Holy Spirit, grant us the strength to follow your example being gracious to others and share in your peace.

In Jesus' precious name, Amen.

∞

Questions
1. Which of Jesus' parables speak mercy into your life?
2. What is the context of the story of Sodom and Gomorrah?
3. Why did Jonah try to run away from God?
4. What should our attitude be about sinners approaching the end times?

GRACE

The Hidden Treasure

> *The kingdom of heaven is like treasure hidden in a field,*
> *which a man found and covered up.*
> *Then in his joy, he goes and sells all that he has*
> *and buys that field.*
> (Matt 13:44)

The second characteristic of God in Exodus 34:6 is grace. Philip Yancy (1997, 14) writes: "Trace the roots of grace, or charis in Greek, and you will find a verb that means 'I rejoice, I am glad.'" If grace is an undeserved blessing, then grace is nowhere more evident than in the healing and resurrection miracles that Jesus performed.

As discussed earlier, grace differs from mercy by implicitly requiring a closer relationship, as will be more obvious in the following discussions.

Resurrection of the Widow's Son

Consider the story of the Widow's son:

> As he drew near to the gate of the town, behold, a man who had died was being carried out, the only son of his mother, and she was a widow, and a considerable crowd from the town was with her. And when the Lord saw her, he had compassion on her and said to her, Do not weep. Then he came up and touched the bier, and the bearers stood still. And he said, Young man, I say to you, arise. And the dead man sat up and began to speak, and Jesus gave him to his mother. (Luke 7:12–15)

We know that this resurrection is an act of unmitigated grace, because the mother and the son have done nothing to deserve this miracle. In fact, we know nothing about them at all from the story, except that the mother is a widow and the dead boy is her only son.

The fact that the widow's child is an only son suggests that the widow is especially destitute in a male-dominated culture—the widow has no one to support or legally defend her. She cannot inherit property and will likely either have to beg or prostitute herself to survive. This story reminds us of Elijah's resurrection of the widow of Zarephath's son (1 Kgs 17) and of God's special concern for widows in general (Exod 22:22).

Needless to say, if the widow is deserving, it is solely because of her status as a widow, not from any action on her own part. In the raising of Lazarus, who was four days dead and buried, this point was even more emphatically emphasized—how much faith did Lazarus have? (Metaxas 2015, 72) We are not told. The resurrection was an act of divine grace, not of mercy or restitution for services rendered. The many healing and resurrection stories found in the Gospels likewise assure us that Jesus is divinely gracious.

Hidden Treasure

Jesus' parable of the Hidden Treasure likewise points to God's grace, but it also suggests that our response to grace is important.

Interestingly, in the parable cited above we are not told what this treasure is. We might envision this story as a man who, on plowing a rented field, digs up a pot full of gold coins. The core idea here is that the treasure in this story is a windfall gain, totally undeserved but that requires further investment to realize the gain.

Just like Bill Gates, I was playing with computers in the early 1970s, but unlike Mr. Gates, I did not undertake investment in computers or envision the development of a personal computer. I was like the man who prayed to God to win the lottery only to hear a voice from heaven advising him to buy a lottery ticket! How many of us have wanted the treasure but have not been willing to risk making an investment?

In case we missed his point, Jesus told a second parable like the first: "Again, the kingdom of heaven is like a merchant in search of fine pearls, who, on finding one pearl of great value, went and sold all that he had and bought it." (Matt 13:45–46). These two parables are then followed by a third parable highlighting

God's judgment.

God does not dispense miracles and grace for naught. Many times God's grace requires action on our part to receive the blessing. It is like the medical student who completes their degree needs to practice medicine to reap the benefit of their training. A miracle is a sign of God's presence in our lives: How will we respond?

∞

Righteous Father,

We praise you for your many miracles and other blessings that we do not deserve.

We confess that we are so undeserving that we do not even recognize when we are blessed. It is like the stock investor who got lucky, but took it as being smart and imprudently lost everything.

Thank you for your willingness to forgive our hardened hearts and clouded minds.

In the power of your Holy Spirit, forgive our ungrateful responses and foolish thoughts. Be patient with us and give us teachable hearts. May our lessons be learned rather than lead to our undoing.

In Jesus's precious name, Amen.

Questions
1. How do you define grace? How does it differ from mercy?
2. Where do we see grace displayed in the New Testament?
3. Where in your life have you found or missed a hidden treasure?
4. Why does grace require a response?

Lost Sheep

> *Go home to your friends*
> *and tell them how much the Lord has done for you,*
> *and how he has had mercy on you.*
> (Mark 5:19)

The idea that grace comes with obligations bothers many Christians, who question any doctrine that they feel is inconsistent with a "loving God." Doctrines like original sin, election, and judgment do not comport well with their image of God. For them, grace means universal salvation, which implies that any obligation imposed by grace is simply unacceptable.

Dietrich Bonhoeffer railed about the problem of "cheap grace," which he defined as:

> The preaching of forgiveness without requiring repentance, baptism without church discipline, Communion without confession, absolution without personal confession. Cheap grace is grace without discipleship, grace without the cross, grace without Jesus Christ, living, and incarnate. (Bonhoeffer 1995, 44–45).

Bonhoeffer is clearly in the minority today because practically every worship service where confessional prayers are offered is immediately followed with a pastoral declaration of universal forgiveness. Worse, influential authors, such as Jack Rogers, have gone so far as to formally advocate for the Bible to be interpreted relative to the double-love command (Matt 24:36–40), disparaging any verse inconsistent with their licentious interpretation of love (Rogers 2009, 65).

Healing of the Man With an Unclean Spirit

Divergent views on God's grace lie at the heart of cultural conflict within the church today. Interpreting Jesus' miracles and parables can offer insight into this conflict.

Consider the healing of the man with an unclean spirit, which appears in the three synoptic Gospels (Matthew, Mark, and Luke), and in each case follows the account of the storm on the Galilee. Mark's version is the longest and offers details of obvious interest to a modern reader.

Only in Mark do we learn that the crossing of the Galilee involved multiple boats and took place in the evening. This may be a reason perhaps why Jesus was sleeping on the boat (Mark 4:35–36). We also learn that this man cuts himself with stones (Mark 5:5), which implies that he was a cutter and likely a teenager.

Our hearts go out to teenagers who cut themselves, an affliction in which emotional pain is so great that physical pain is easier to bear. This man was likely abused or went through some other trauma, like being a child soldier or an orphan. Mark's account leaves us with a much different impression than Luke or Matthew's, where the man is described as demon possessed. It may also suggest why Jesus may have gone out of his way to heal this man.

Grace in the Mark and Luke accounts includes the stipulation cited above (Mark 5:19). The man is healed and is immediately commissioned by Jesus to evangelize the people of the Decapolis region. The Decapolis was named for ten independent, Roman cities (Mark 5:20). This is a remarkable request because the only knowledge this man had of Jesus was his own healing and the entire region was predominantly gentile, not Jewish. The herding of pigs, which plays an important role in this man's healing, was largely unknown among Jews because of dietary restrictions.

Parable of the Lost Sheep

While grace in the healing of the man with the unclean spirit was followed by a request that the man evangelize his home town, the Parable of the Lost Sheep provides an important counter example. Consider the parable again:

> What man of you, having a hundred sheep, if he has lost one of them, does not leave the ninety-nine in the open country, and go after the one that is lost, until he finds it? And when he has found it, he lays it on his shoulders, rejoicing. And when he comes home, he

calls together his friends and his neighbors, saying to them, Rejoice with me, for I have found my sheep that was lost. Just so, I tell you, there will be more joy in heaven over one sinner who repents than over ninety-nine righteous persons who need no repentance. (Luke 15:4–7)

One reading of this parable is that sheep cannot be expected to respond to their recovery by the shepherd, as in the case of the man with the unclean spirit. It seems to be forgiveness without repentance.

A subtler reading of this passage arises when Jesus refers to his followers as his flock. Jesus says in his sermon: "When he [the Good Shepherd] has brought out all his own, he goes before them, and the sheep follow him, for they know his voice, … I am the good shepherd. I know my own and my own know me." (John 10:4, 14) The inference here is that grace is followed by faith among those elected for salvation.

Healing of the Ten Lepers

We see this response in the healing of the ten lepers (Luke 17:12–19). Jesus said:

Go and show yourselves to the priests. And as they went they were cleansed. Then one of them, when he saw that he was healed, turned back, praising God with a loud voice; and he fell on his face at Jesus' feet, giving him thanks. Now he was a Samaritan. (Luke 17:14–16)

What is interesting here is that the healing required a stipulation:

"Go and show yourselves to the priests." There is also a response: The Samaritan returned to thank Jesus, which is described as an act of faith. All ten were healed, but only one displayed faith.

We have recently experienced a similar healing. In 2021, researchers developed a vaccine for corona virus in less than a year. This development was unprecedented and may have saved millions of lives worldwide. Was this just another scientific discovery or was it the hand of God at work in our generation? Myself, I have frequently described scientific advancements as God's Easter eggs—little treats that we hide where we know our children will find them.

∞

Beloved Lord Jesus,

We praise you for your life of service, your death on the cross, and your resurrection to give us the hope of salvation.

Forgive us when we fail to model your sacrificial life and neglect to share your love with those around us.

Thank you for the many blessings of this life, including life, health, family, and work.

In the power of your Holy Spirit, grant us strength for sacrificial living, grace for those we meet, and the peace that passes all understanding.

In Jesus' precious name, Amen.

∞

Questions
1. What is cheap grace? Why has grace become controversial in the church?
2. Where did the man with the unclean spirit live? Why is it interesting?
3. What is a cutter? Why does this change our view of this healing?
4. Why does it matter what a sheep is in Jesus' parable of the Lost Sheep?

Sin as Sickness

> *Those who are well have no need of a physician,*
> *but those who are sick.*
> *I have not come to call the righteous*
> *but sinners to repentance.*
> (Luke 5:31–32)

Jesus' Parable of the Doctor and the Sick is found in three Gospels (Mark 2:17, Matt 9:12–13, Luke 5:31–32). In each case, the parable is paired with a statement about his mission: "I have not come to call the righteous but sinners to repentance." This pairing converts the parable into a doublet, a form of Hebrew poetry, where the first phrase is rephrased by the second. In other words, the healthy are righteous while the sick are sinners. Jesus' role in this parable doublet is that of a physician.

We witness another example of this pairing of healing and forgiveness of sin in the healing of the paralytic, also found in three Gospels (Mark 2:9, Matt 9:5, Luke 5:23) and in each case found close to the Parable of the Doctor and the Sick. The key phrase in each account is: "Which is easier, to say to the paralytic, your sins are forgiven, or to say, rise, take up your bed and walk?" (Mark 2:9) The argument is from the greater (physical healing) to the lesser (forgiveness of sin). The question is rhetorical because Jesus already knows what he will do.

The grace extended to the paralytic serves an important didactical point: Jesus has the power to forgive sins, as suggested in the Parable of the Doctor and the Sick (Luke 5:32). This is a claim to divinity, as noted in Mark's Gospel: "Who can forgive sins but God alone?" (Mark 2:7) This is an example of a miracle functioning as a sign of God's presence because only gracious and a loving God would countermand the rules of the universe to heal someone. The only request made of the paralytic was to: "Rise, pick up your bed and go home." (Luke 5:24)

Sin as an Illness

It is interesting that Jesus treats sin as an illness, much like the modern parallel of treating addictions as an illness. If sin is an illness, then the shame is relinquished and the sinner is allowed to accept forgiveness. Shame is normally a barrier to healing and forgiveness as those responsible are excluded from normal relationships with family and community.

Georges (2017, 10–11) sees three spiritual cultures that appear as responses to sin: guilt, shame, and fear:

1. Guilt-innocence cultures that focus on an individual's response to law breaking and the pursuit of justice.
2. Shame-honor cultures that focus on fulfilling group expectations and restoring honor when norms are

violated.

3. Fear-power cultures that focus on fear of evil and seek power over the spiritual world through magic, spells, curses, and rituals.

Treating sin as a sickness in a guilt-innocence culture relieves one of a legal violation. In an shame-honor culture one is relieved of shame. In a fear-power culture one is relieved of a curse. In each case, treating sin as an illness allows healing to take place that might otherwise not be possible, as those in power lose their claim over the sinner.

The impact of treating sin as an illness is particularly important in dealing with besetting sins. These are sins with the characteristics of addiction that trap and enslave us over long periods of time. Here we find things like sexual sins, sins involving money and power over others, and attitudes that preclude forgiveness.

Seeing Jesus as a dispenser of grace, healing, and forgiveness places him at a cultural-spiritual vortex, where the power structure of the culture is threatened. When Jesus offers grace, heals, and forgives, those normally responsible for such activities are deprived of their usual status and can be expected to lash out in response. It is no wonder that Jesus' life was in danger the more real his healing miracles became (e.g. Mark 3:1–6).

∞

Almighty God, Great Physician, Spirit of Truth,

All power and dominion, honor and glory, and truth and justice are yours because you hear our afflictions, heal our diseases, and free us from fear. Be ever near.

Forgive our weaknesses, our gullibility, and inability to say no to sin. Be ever near.

Thank you for the many blessings, the blessings we see, and the blessings hid from our eyes when we are simply faithful. Be ever near.

In the power of your Holy Spirit, turn our eyes away from sin, heal our bodies, and bring us closer to you in good times and bad.

In Jesus' precious name, Amen.

∞

Questions
1. Why is Jesus' treatment of sin as illness so powerful?
2. What are three types of spiritual cultures?
3. What is a besetting sin?
4. What is a parable doublet?

Contending Grace

> *No servant can serve two masters,*
> *for either he will hate the one and love the other,*
> *or he will be devoted to the one and despise the other.*
> *You cannot serve God and money.*
> (Luke 16:13)

*L*azarus and the Rich Man is a parable in the form of a lengthy story of two men: a poor beggar named Lazarus and a rich man, who is not named. This parable appears only in Luke 16 and it follows another story about an unfaithful and unscrupulous manager. This prior story concludes with the above proverbial statement: You cannot serve God and money. The context of this prior story suggests that money-obsessed Pharisees are the ones in view being criticized in the above story. The rich man in the parable is also criticized.

If grace is an undeserved blessing, then the Parable of Lazarus and the Rich Man is a story of contending acts of grace. We read:

> There was a rich man who was clothed in purple and fine linen and who feasted sumptuously every day. And at his gate was laid a poor man named Lazarus, covered with sores. (Luke 16:19–20)

Neither acts of God's sovereign grace are initially explained, but we learn more about the rich man as the story unfolds. We read:

> The poor man died and was carried by the angels to Abraham's side. The rich man also died and was buried, and in Hades, being in torment, he lifted up his eyes and saw Abraham far off and Lazarus at his side. (Luke 16:22-23)

We sense bewilderment in the rich man's eyes as he looks up from Hades to Lazarus enjoying Abraham's bosom. This role reversal is unexpected and comes as a shock. The rich man questions Abraham and asks him to warn his five brothers. Abraham responds: "They have Moses and the Prophets; let them hear them." (Luke 16:29)

Curiously, we are never told why Lazarus warranted heaven, only that the rich man failed to heed Moses and the Prophets' teaching on how to deal with divine judgment. Given the context of the parable, however, we can surmise that we are to love God, not money (Luke 16:13), unlike the Pharisees. The quality of our relationship with God is the key.

Grace in the Parable

For Lazarus, grace means a reversal of fortunes in death. God takes pity on him in death for his undeserved suffering in life. This is a common expectation of what it means to go to heaven.

For the rich man, grace means prosperity in life with the caveat that he love God, not money, and heed Moses and the Prophets. This expectation of divine judgment is rejected by most people today, who prefer to believe in universal salvation.

The story is silent on Lazarus' relationship with God and attitude towards Moses and the Prophets. This reinforces the perception that the parable is directed at and critical of the Pharisees, as with the prior story.

Grace in Relationship

The idea that God's grace is dispensed in the context of relationship is explicit in the Parable of the Two Sons, usually called the Parable of the Prodigal Son. In the parable, the younger son asks for his inheritance early and uses it to engage in riotous living in a foreign country while the old son remains at home and works for this father. At this point, neither son loves his father.

After ending up destitute, the younger son returns home to ask his father's forgiveness. This leaves the older son even more bitter, both at his brother and at his father for accepting him back. For the younger son, this episode represents a coming-of-age story where he learns to love his father, something that his older brother never manages (Luke 15:11–32).

In the Parable of the Two Sons, the father models God's grace in two archetypal cases represented by the two sons. In both cases, the father offers restorative justice—grace designed to allow growth—where he might have rendered criminal justice, had the sons not been in relationship.

Restorative justice makes sense to Christians because many of us have known Christ our entire lives, but it was new to Jesus' audience. The expectation at that point was: "This our son is stubborn and rebellious; he will not obey our voice; he is a glutton and a drunkard. Then all the men of the city shall stone him to death with stones." (Deut 21:20–21) One reading of the passage—"but while he was still a long way off, his father saw him and felt compassion, and ran and embraced him and kissed him." (Luke 15:20)—is that the father was protecting his son from a community more accustomed to stoning rebellious sons, an example of criminal justice, than offering them restorative justice. Against this backdrop, the father's response is unexpected, a radical departure from local custom.

The grace that Jesus displays in the Parable of the Prodigal Son is culturally unexpected. It is transformative because it allows renewal of relationship and the opportunity of personal growth. Because the church has typically interpreted this parable allegorically, the father is a stand-in for God and we are expected to identify with the younger son. The renewed relationship is therefore seen to be our relationship with God, and by inference, a model for our relationship with everyone else.

∞

Father God,

All praise and honor, power and glory, truth and justice are yours, because you offer us shelter that allows us to grow and become adults in a world more accustomed to stunted youths and bitter relationships. Be ever near.

Forgive us our youthful arrogance, our prideful rebellion, and our wanton covetousness.

Thank you for the gift of your son, our savior Jesus Christ, who lived teaching us to love one another, healed our wounds, died on the cross for our sins, and rose again from the dead that we might have life.

In the power of your Holy Spirit, teach us to model the grace and love of Jesus Christ to all that we meet. Grant us a spirit of truth and holiness.

In Jesus' precious name, Amen.

∞

Questions
1. Who was Lazarus?
2. Why was the rich man surprised at his status in death?
3. What is restorative justice? How does it differ from criminal justice?
4. Why is the father's acceptance of the Prodigal Son surprising?

Applying Grace

> *While we were still sinners, Christ died for us.*
> (Rom 5:8)

In the parables examined, we begin to see the nature of God's grace.

While God's grace is an undeserved blessing, Jesus' parable of the Hidden Treasure suggests that our response to grace is important (Matt 13:44). Much like a spiritual gift, a gracious blessing is of little use if we hide it away and make no use of it. It is as though we have been given tomorrow's stock report, but we neglect to purchase shares to take advantage of the insight.

Responding to God's grace is important in understanding the Parable of the Lost Sheep. Lost sheep are more likely to be found if they listen for the shepherd's voice. Jesus said: "I am the good shepherd. I know my own and my own know me." (John 10:14) As in the healing of the Ten Lepers, it is important to follow the shepherd's instructions: "Go and show yourselves to the priest." (Luke 17:14)

In the Parable of the Doctor and the Sick, we find Jesus graciously treating sin as an illness (Luke 5:31–32). This re-imaging of sin removes sin's guilt, shame, and curse to heal our hearts and our relationships. This makes reformation and change possible.

The Parable of Lazarus and the Rich Man in Luke 16 displays grace in different contexts, both in life and in the afterlife. The fault of the rich man is that he failed to give thanks to God for his blessings in this life and did not prepare for the afterlife.

In the Parable of the Two Sons, we see God using grace to enable the prodigal son to find the error of his ways and grow to love his father. (Luke 15:11–32) This parable speaks to our own reunion with God made possible by Jesus' death on the cross.

In each of these parables, we see God using grace strategically to encourage, lead, and grow us in the context of relationship. This is not the cheap grace that Bonhoeffer (1995, 44–45) railed against. Rather, the picture that the parables and healing stories paint of grace is of an activist (immanent) God who intervenes in our lives. Jesus' God is not detached or aloof (transcendent), like a puppeteer or a man behind the curtain. He is the caring father who attends all our performances and our games, quietly watching and encouraging us to reach our potential.

Magnified Grace

The two most significant examples of God's grace are our creation and salvation in Jesus Christ that took place long before our birth for which we cannot be said to be deserving.

While creation is often seen as an historical event in the distant past, it is also a personal event in our own lives. We are created male and female in God's own image, an image now displayed in the life and ministry of Jesus Christ. Spiritual gifts are uniquely personal and they shape our destinies. We are not hatched in an incubator by a distant or non-existent deity, subject to random influences and forces. Our creation is one of God's most gracious acts.

Our salvation through Jesus' death on the cross is another undeserved act of God's grace. The Apostle Paul says it best:

> For while we were still weak, at the right time Christ died for the ungodly. For one will scarcely die for a righteous person—though perhaps for a good person one would dare even to die—but God shows his love for us in that while we were still sinners, Christ died for us. (Rom 5:6–8)

God's sacrificial grace takes place in the context of relationship, because God does not leave us alone, but like sheep we need to recognize and follow the shepherd.

God's grace is like rain that is easy to take for granted, but absolutely crucial for life—especially if you are a farmer—and desperately missed when it is absent.

∞

Gracious Father,

All honor and glory, power and dominion, truth and justice are yours, for you created us out of dust and redeemed us with Christ's death on the cross. Be ever near.

Forgive us for our poor stewardship of your creation and denial of your salvation. Remind us of your presence.

Thank you for the spiritual gifts that you have given us, the favorable weather with which you have blessed us, and the example of your son.

In the power of your Holy Spirit, lift the pandemic that has plagued us, order the chaos that engulfs our leaders, and remove the wanton spirit of conflict that has thrown its shadow over us. May we grow to reflect your grace to those we live with and meet every day.

In Jesus' precious name, Amen.

∞

Questions
1. What is your favorite example of grace in the New Testament?
2. Why are the healing miracles of Jesus a sign of his grace?
3. What are the two most important acts of God's grace?
4. What is your favorite parable of grace?

PATIENCE

Two Builders

> *Whoever is slow to anger has great understanding,*
> *but he who has a hasty temper exalts folly.*
> (Prov 14:29)

The third characteristic of God in Exodus 34:6 is patience. The Hebrew words used here *areke affaim* (אֶ֥רֶךְ אַפַּ֖יִם,), literally mean long nostrilled. The words are often translated as slow to anger (ESV) or long suffering (KJV). Think of the person who takes a deep breath and counts to ten before responding to an insult. The Septuagint Greek translates this expression as *macrothymos* (μακρόθυμος), which means "being self-controlled in the face of provocation, patient, forbearing, tolerant, even-tempered." (BDAG 4685) By itself, the word for nostril is used in paying respect by bowing, a more positive inference in the Hebrew (e.g. Gen 19:1). Proverbs equates such patience with great understanding or wisdom, the opposite of which is folly (Prov 14:29).

Patience as Paradigm

Two aspects of patience, wisdom and time, characterize many of Jesus' parables.

A wisdom theme pervades virtually all of Jesus' parables in the sense of: "The fear of the LORD is the beginning of knowledge; fools despise wisdom and instruction." (Prov

1:7) Consistent with the definition of a parable in both Greek and Hebrew, a parable imparts wisdom, much like Solomon's proverbs. Jesus' parables have the special characteristic of also pointing the listener to God, which firmly places them in the Bible's wisdom literature.

The time aspect of patience has a think-before-you-speak flavor. Consider the Parable of the Two Builders found in Matthew and Luke:

> Everyone who comes to me and hears my words and does them, I will show you what he is like: he is like a man building a house, who dug deep and laid the foundation on the rock. And when a flood arose, the stream broke against that house and could not shake it, because it had been well built. But the one who hears and does not do them is like a man who built a house on the ground without a foundation. When the stream broke against it, immediately it fell, and the ruin of that house was great. (Luke 6:47–49)

The time aspect of the parable arises in anticipating future events, in this case a flood, that reinforces the wisdom aspect. Even today, we can see many homes built on flood plains and ocean sandbars only later to be inundated and destroyed.

Patience's Eschatological Dimension

While the Parable of the Two Builders clearly captures wisdom common in the building trades of everyday life, it also has an eschatological character to it. In the Bible, a house can refer to a family tree or dynasty. Eschatology has to do with the end times as described in scripture. In the parable, Jesus compares someone who listens to his teaching as the builder, implying that Jesus is himself the rock on which the house is to be built. The flood in this parable is easily a metaphor for death, as in the flood of Noah (Gen 7) where the house is presumably all of humanity that descended from Noah's line.

In for a penny, in for a pound: Patience is the root of eschatology. Because God created the heavens and the earth (Gen 1), time will also have an end when Christ will return. Many of Jesus' parables call for us to anticipate his return. While Christ's return has a future aspect, it informs how we are to live today. Because we know life's story will have a happy ending, we need not worry and can take risks for the kingdom today.

Patience's Practical Application

While many people lampoon Christianity as pie in the sky, faith promotes patience and research shows that children who are patient today are much more likely to succeed in life.

Walter Mischel explored the mystery of patience among four year olds. Those willing to forgo a single treat now in deference to two in twenty minutes are substantially more likely to succeed in life even years later. Mischel (2014, 3) reports:

The more seconds they waited at age four or five, the higher their SAT scores and the better their rated social and cognitive functioning in adolescence. At age 27–32, those who had waited longer during the Marshmallow Test in preschool had lower body mass index and a better sense of self-worth, pursued their goals more effectively, and coped more adaptively with frustration and stress.

These impressive results at an early age suggest that patience is a valuable characteristic that can presumably be taught or learned by simply imitating Jesus.

∞

Patient and Loving Father,

All praise and honor, power and dominion, truth and justice are yours, because you created the heavens and the earth and will one day return to bring us home.

We confess that we do not always wait patiently for your answers in prayer or act as if we believe in your return in the eschaton (end times). Teach us patience.

Thank you for our creation and the many spiritual gifts that you have given us.

In the power of your Holy Spirit, grant us your holy patience that we might live expectantly that when life blesses us with opportunities, we might be ready to take advantage of them.

In Jesus' precious name, Amen.

Questions
1. How does the Hebrew in Exodus 34:6 describe patience?
2. What two aspects of patience can you name?
3. What does patience have to do with the eschaton?
4. What is the Marshmallow Test?

The Sower

> *As for that in the good soil, they are those who,*
> *hearing the word, hold it fast in an honest*
> *and good heart, and bear fruit with patience.*
> *(Luke 8:15)*

Patience engenders a heart of faith.

In the Parable of the Sower, found in Matthew 13:3–23, Mark 4:3–20, and Luke 8:5–15, Jesus likens himself to a farmer sowing seed:

> A sower went out to sow. And as he sowed, some seeds fell along the path, and the birds came and devoured them. Other seeds fell on rocky ground, where they did not have much soil, and immediately they sprang up, since they had no depth of soil, but when the sun rose they were scorched. And since they had no root, they withered away. Other seeds fell among thorns, and the thorns grew up and choked them. Other seeds fell on good soil and produced grain, some a hundredfold, some sixty, some thirty. He who has ears, let him hear. (Matt 13:3–9)

The life of the farmer starts and ends with a patient heart. In the rocky soil of Palestine, it is not always obvious where one will dig up a stone, which makes planting a crap-shoot. Neither is the weather reliable and predictable. Modern Israel has lush crops, but only where irrigation is available. Time and patience are requisite for a farmer to gain a harvest.

In further discussion, Jesus explains that the soil in this

parable is the word of God (e.g. Luke 8:11), which makes this parable an allegory. Substituting that the revealed context of the parable is the preaching of the word of God clarifies the meaning of the parable.

The Character of Patience

You may be wondering why I chose to talk about patience in the Parable of the Sower. The parable is not about patience; the parable is about the character of good and bad soil (Matt 13:19-23). The reason is this—there is no such thing as an impatient farmer. One cannot be a farmer without patience. Farming requires patience. The parable assumes that the farmer is patient, which allows a story to then be told about soils. Not coincidentally, time and patience are also required to be a good parent, one of the chief characteristics of God that Jesus leaves us with.

The Parable of the Wheat and the Tares

The Matthew account of the Parable of the Sower is followed immediately by a second farming story, the Parable of the Wheat and the Tares. A tare (KJV) is a weed with poisonous seeds that resembles wheat called darnel (*zizanion*, BDAG 3384). Roman law specifically forbad the sowing of darnel in the wheat fields of an enemy, suggesting that this parable is based on a nasty ancient practice (Keener 2009, 386–387) Matthew writes:

> The kingdom of heaven may be compared to a man who sowed good seed in his field, but while his men were sleeping, his enemy came and sowed weeds among the wheat and went away. So when the plants came up and bore grain, then the weeds appeared also. And the servants of the master of the house came and said to him, Master, did you not sow good seed in your field? How then does it have weeds? He said to them, An enemy has done this. So the servants said to him, Then do you want us to go and gather them? But he said, No, lest in gathering the weeds you root up the wheat along with them. Let both grow together until the harvest, and at harvest time I will tell the reapers, Gather the weeds first and bind them in bundles to be burned, but gather the wheat into my barn. (Matt 13:24–30)

In the parable, the master of the house specifically directs his servants not to pull the weeds, lest the wheat get pulled up as well. This direction requires the servants to be patient to allow the wheat to grow.

The fruit of patience in this parable is faith, which is engendered by a teachable heart. The eschatological judgment of God is deferred, we surmise, so that the faithful can be revealed and the unfaithful winnowed out. Patience has its limits in the parable as the winnowing is done at the time of harvest.

∞

Most patient father,

All praise and honor, power and dominion, truth and justice are yours because you are the gracious father who gives us time to grow and models the image that we are to grow into.

Forgive our impatience. Overlook our youth. Heal our sinful hearts for we are unable to pattern our lives after Christ without your assistance.

Thank you for times and seasons of life when we can take tiny steps in your direction and help others to follow.

In the power of your Holy Spirit, shelter your church and our lives from the winds of mindless change that wash away the legacy of the faithful that proceeded us. Grant us the strength rather to build your legacy with the time that you have given us, and bless us with a revival of faith in this generation.

In Jesus' precious name, Amen.

∞

Questions
1. Why do farming illustrations model patience?
2. What is a tare? What is darnel?
3. What is a fruit of patience?
4. Why does God defer judgment?

The Talents

> *Teach us to number our days*
> *that we may get a heart of wisdom.*
> (Ps 90:12)

*J*esus teaches us to watch for his return, a mark of patience. Mark 13:33 reads: "Take heed, keep on the alert; for you do not know when the appointed time will come." Likewise, Luke 12:35 echoes the Parable of the Ten Virgins: "Be dressed in readiness, and keep your lamps lit." Directly after the Parable of the Ten Virgins in Matthew 25, we read the Parable of the Talents that not only advises watchfulness, but guides us on how to center our lives on God as we wait.

Risk-taking for Christ

The Parable of the Talents starts with advice about being watchful, but then goes on:

> For it will be like a man going on a journey, who called his servants and entrusted to them his property. To one he gave five talents, to another two, to another one, to each according to his ability. Then he went away. (Matt 25:14–15)

We are then told how the first two servants invested the master's money and doubled his principal, while the third servant buried the master's money in the ground.

When the master returns, he settles accounts with each

of the servants. The first two servants present the master with his principal and the earnings from their investments. In both cases, the master responds with the same statement: "Well done, good and faithful servant. You have been faithful over a little; I will set you over much. Enter into the joy of your master." (Matt 25:21)

In contrast to the first two servants' risk-taking, the third servant acts out of fear:

> Master, I knew you to be a hard man, reaping where you did not sow, and gathering where you scattered no seed, so I was afraid, and I went and hid your talent in the ground. Here, you have what is yours. (Matt 25:24–25)

The master calls this servant "wicked and slothful" and parrots the servant's suggestion that he is a hard man, suggesting agreement, but he goes on: "Then you ought to have invested my money with the bankers, and at my coming I should have received what was my own with interest." (Matt 25:27)

In so many words, the master suggests that the third servant is both cowardly and imprudent, because depositing the money with a banker requires accepting little risk of financial loss. The master takes the money given to the third servant and gives it to the first. Then, the third servant is described as worthless and condemned to perdition, a penalty too harsh for most postmodern people even to hear.

Lessons on Waiting

What do we learn from this parable? The first thing to note is the context. Immediately after the Parable of the Talents is another parable of judgment, where the goats and the sheep are separated. Then, in chapter 26 of Matthew, we read:

> When Jesus had finished all these sayings, he said to his disciples, You know that after two days the Passover is coming, and the Son of Man will be delivered up to be crucified. (Matt 26:1–2)

The implication is that the three parables in chapter 25 are given to prepare the disciples for Jesus' death, resurrection, and second coming. All three suggest that the disciples should be watchful of Christ's return, but only the Parable of the Talents suggests how to spend the time while Jesus is absent.

Knowing that Christ will return, the parable suggests that we should be cheerful, not fearful, in our work, taking risks to advance the Kingdom of God. It is like the roulette player who knows what the next number will be: The bet measures confidence in the knowledge, determines the level of winnings, and suggests an appropriate attitude. Christ's good and faithful servants are described as cheerful risk-takers rather than fearful hoarders, who confidently invest the king's resources to earn the highest returns.

God of Abundance

Schlossberg (1990, 316) writes: "A steward is the caretaker of property that belongs to another. A good steward husbands the property and causes it to produce its proper income." In the Parable of the Talents (Matt 25:14–29), Jesus pictures the good steward as not only earning income (depositing with a banker), but also taking risks to invest the property and earn above-average returns (doubling property value). By contrast, the bad steward allows the property to depreciate, which is the immediate consequence of hoarding during inflation.

This last point is crucial. We serve a God of abundance. In John's Gospel (2, 6, 21), we see a God who multiplies wine, bread, and fish far beyond expectations. When we model our lives on this God, we expect to be generous and take risks for the kingdom because that is the image of God we are given and we want to be like God.

∞

Wise and loving father,

All praise and honor, power and dominion, truth and justice are yours, because you teach us patience when the world models imprudent impatience that leads to poverty, loneliness, and strife.

We confess that we want the world to gift us with riches, honors, and opportunities without effort, delay, or investment. We do not want delay or advice that would bring the things that we desire.

Thanks be to you for you are patient with us and sit with us like a loving parent while we wait.

In the power of your Holy Spirit, guard our hearts so that "neither death nor life, nor angels nor rulers, nor things present nor things to come, nor powers, nor height nor depth, nor anything else in all creation, will be able to separate us from the love of God in Christ Jesus our Lord." (Rom 8:38–39)

In Jesus' precious name, Amen.

∞

Questions
1. What is the mark of patience in the Christian?
2. How should we spend our time as we wait on Christ's return?
3. What should our attitude be in our work?
4. How does the Gospel of John picture God?

Ten Virgins

> *Therefore you also must be ready,*
> *for the Son of Man is coming*
> *at an hour you do not expect.*
> (Matt 24:44)

The Olivet Discourse (e.g. Mark 13; Matt 24) describes prophetic statements that Jesus shares with his disciples just before his arrest and crucifixion as they stood on the Mount of Olives and viewed Jerusalem. Prophecy is often taken as a forecasting activity that describes future events, but Jesus almost always talks about the future as a way to motivate how life should be lived today. Two words that describe how to live today might be: Patient expectation. Theologians talk about the Kingdom of God being both already here and not yet (Ladd 1991, 68–69). The word *proleptic* captures this idea where the future is revealed today (Ferguson 1997, 177).

Olivet Discourse

Consider this brief part of the Olivet Discourse:

> Therefore you also must be ready, for the Son of Man is coming at an hour you do not expect. Who then is the faithful and wise servant, whom his master has set over his household, to give them their food at the proper time? Blessed is that servant whom his master will find so doing when he comes. (Matt 24:44–46)

Here Jesus counsels his disciples to watch for his return, patiently attending to household duties and not chasing after various crises that he itemizes:

> And you will hear of wars and rumors of wars. See that you are not alarmed, for this must take place, but the end is not yet. For nation will rise against nation, and kingdom against kingdom, and there will be famines and earthquakes in various places. (Matt 24:6–7)

This message is repeated over and over in the Olivet Discourse, Jesus' most lengthy prophetic statement. Patient expectation suggests being aware of the times and seasons, but not losing one's head the midst of chaos. The focus in the Olivet Discourse is on faithfully attending to one's duties as Christ's disciples, not obsessing about current or future crises, fantastic prophesies, or the second coming.

Old Testament Prophecy

In the Old Testament, we see two kinds of prophets: Covenantal prophets and covenant-lawsuit prophets. Covenantal prophets are like Moses and Nathan who interact with God to introduce new covenants. When Moses receives the Ten Commandments on Mount Sinai (Exod 20) or Nathan shares his dream with King David (2 Sam 7), they are functioning as covenantal prophets. Covenant-lawsuit prophets, like Elijah and Elisha, remind the people and their king of their obligations under the covenant, especially the blessings and curses found in Deuteronomy 28. While the covenant-lawsuit prophets who prophesy fire and brimstone gather the most attention, Jesus clearly functioned as both types of prophets in the Olivet Discourse.

One of the key statements of the role of a prophet distinguishes Moses from prophets who are only given visions and dreams:

> Hear my words: If there is a prophet among you, I the LORD make myself known to him in a vision; I speak with him in a dream. Not so with my servant Moses. He is faithful in all my house. With him I speak mouth to mouth, clearly, and not in riddles, and he beholds the form of the LORD. Why then were you not afraid to speak against my servant Moses? (Num 12:6–8)

Here the prophet only repeats the words given him by God, whether received in a vision or in person. More generally, the idea of a prophet as a soothsayer, fortune teller, or forecaster of future events motivates the Greek word *prophet*. More typically in the New Testament, the preferred reference to the prophetic role is Apostle, which means messenger or one who is sent, to avoid confusion with the Greek concept of a prophet.

The focus of the Old Testament prophet is on adhering to the covenant, not on forecasting future events. This suggests that the Old Testament prophet and the New Testament prophet share a common focus on patiently adhering to a faithful lifestyle, especially in confusing times.

The Parable of the Ten Virgins

We see this prophetic framework modeled in the Parable of the Ten Virgins: "Then the kingdom of heaven will be like ten virgins who took their lamps and went to meet the bridegroom." (Matt 25:1) The wise virgins brought extra oil; the foolish did not. When the bridegroom is delayed, the foolish virgin's lamps ran out of oil and they were excluded from the wedding, an analogy to heaven. In this parable, patience is modeled in the idea of being prepared for whatever comes to pass.

The parable is more widely an analogy to the language of Revelation where the church is described as the bride of Christ, who is the bridegroom: "Let us rejoice and exult and give him the glory, for the marriage of the Lamb has come, and his Bride has made herself ready." (Rev 19:7) The importance of the marriage feast of the Lamb to Christian eschatology places the character trait of patience—one of the Apostle Paul's fruits of the spirit (Gal 5:22)—at the heart of the Gospel.

∞

Almighty Father,

All praise and honor, power and dominion, truth and

justice are yours, because you teach how to live today with stories about the future.

Forgive us our unwillingness to listen, to reform our lives in view of your teaching, and to share our lessons with those around us.

Thank you for the example of Jesus Christ who spoke in parables to inform us about your person and the things we need to know to grow closer to you.

In the power of the Holy Spirit, guide us on the path to salvation today, tomorrow, and always.

In Jesus' precious name, Amen.

∞

Questions
1. What is the Olivet Discourse?
2. How does Jesus talk about the future and prophecy?
3. What are the two types of Old Testament prophets?
4. What is the focus of the Parable of the Ten Virgins?

Applying Patience

> *You also, be patient. Establish your hearts,*
> *for the coming of the Lord is at hand.*
> (Jas 5:8)

In the parables examined, we begin to see the importance of God's patience.

In the Parable of the Two Builders, we find patience associated with good planning and expert workmanship. The expert builder plans for the flood that, though unexpected, is expected over the long haul. Laying a foundation on a rock speaks directly to the current concern about global warming because greater turbulence in weather is at the heart of the concern. More generally, building on the rock of our salvation speaks to attending to our walk of faith with the Lord.

In the Parable of the Sower, we see that the occupation of the farmer requires patience. Farming requires patient planning and a willingness to invest time and effort in a crop that is from the outset hidden. What impatient person would save the seed from the previous harvest, prepare the soil, weed around the plants, and wait for months for a new harvest?

In the Parable of the Talents, we learn to take risks to advance the Kingdom of God while we wait patiently for the Lord's return. Attitude matters. A fearful person is not likely to take risks for an uncertain outcome and the rate of return is substantially diminished because of their fear. God's abundant generosity allays our fear and permits us to prosper in good times and bad.

In the Parable of the Ten Virgins, we again see the need to plan patiently for every contingency. The urgency of our patient planning is shown to be the key to entrance into the wedding feast, a metaphor for heaven. Anyone who has helped prepare a wedding can attest to the eagerness and foolishness of emotionally-charged young people. Even in periods of utter spontaneity, we are cautioned to plan ahead.

The importance of patience and planning for the future in the faith suggests why Christians have always valued and invested more in education than other groups.

Patience in the Early Church

Lessons about patience played an important role in the history of the church. Alan Kreider (2016, 1–2) observes:

> "Patience was not a virtue dear to most Greco-Roman people and it has been of little interest to scholars of early Christianity. But it was centrally important to early Christians, … The sources rarely indicate that the early Christians grew in number because they won arguments, instead they grew because their habitual behavior (rooted in patience) was distinctive and intriguing. Their habitus … enabled them to address

intractable problems that ordinary people faced in ways that offered hope."

Think about it. The upper class of Roman society was known, not for patience, but for drunken orgies. In such a society, people offering sober, patient assistance to those victimized by such leaders would stand out and garner admiration. Kreider (2016, 19) writes:

> When people seek to follow Christ, according to Origen, God forms them into people who embody this patience. Christ's followers are not in a hurry; they listen carefully as the word is read and preached, and they patiently call to account straying Christians who attend worship services irregularly. Patient believers trust God. When they are subjected to penitential discipline, they patiently bear the judgments made about them, where they have been rightly or wrongly deposed.

The nature of Christian worship is to engender patience and habits that improve daily life.

While worship can impart good habits, Donald Dayton (2005, 122–123) observed that periods of revival of the faith are often followed by reversals as "children growing up under such restraints experience them primarily as factors aliening them from their peers and society." In seminary, I noticed a stark difference in the attitude of preachers' kids from missionaries' kids in which the preachers' kids exhibited the response noted by Dayton while the missionaries' kids more clearly witnessed the fruit of their parent's sacrifices and developed a strong faith of their own.

Current Backsliding

If modeling God's patience is of immediate personal benefit, as demonstrated in research associated with the Marshmallow Test, and of long-term benefit to the church, as argued in Kreider's study of the early church, why is our society so negligent in teaching personal discipline to our own children? This backsliding on patience can be attributed to the influence of cell phones and advertising to promote mindless purchasing. Or it may be simply a byproduct of inattention and parental prioritizing of other goals.

One way or another, the impatience that we routinely observe today is clearly detrimental to the spiritual life and to the prudence use of resources in daily living.

Example of Saint Augustine

Rather than end this reflection on a sour note, let me turn back the clock to another period when impatience seemed rampant.

Saint Augustine lived in the fourth century in North Africa and was the model of crass Roman debauchery by his own admission as a young man. Augustine (Foley 2006, 10) pictures himself as an initially lazy student who received frequent beatings, but we are quickly introduced to a pious Monica, his mother, who, seeing her son engaging in self-destructive and sinful behavior, resorted to unceasing prayer. Augustine writes:

> The mother of my flesh was in heavy anxiety, since with a heart chaste in Your faith she was ever in deep travail for my eternal salvation, and would have proceeded without delay to have me consecrated and washed clean by the Sacrament of salvation. (Foley 2006, 12)

Still, it is paradoxical to observe one of the great philosophers of the church saying: "I disliked learning and hated to be forced to it." (Foley 2006, 13) Although Augustine was schooled in rhetoric, like today's attorneys, he was by his own admission not converted to the Christian faith with arguments, but by the patient prayers of a devout mother, Monica.

∞

Loving father,

All glory and honor, power and dominion, truth and justice are yours, because you created us ex-nihilo, out of nothing, and, when we strayed, you patiently sent your son, Jesus Christ, to rescue us from our brokenness and sin, like the patient prayer of Saint Augustine's mother, Monica.

Forgive our impatience, our unwillingness, to follow

your example and our perennial blaming of you for bad choices that we have made.

Thank you for your many blessings and your patient willingness to offer us light in the nighttime of our obstinate youth.

In the power of your Holy Spirit, turn our hearts to your example of patience. Remove the blinders of failing youth and grant us eyes that see, ears that hear, and hands that serve in the midst of much hardship.

In Jesus' precious name, Amen.

∞

Questions
1. Which of Jesus' parables are most memorable to you when it comes to patience?
2. Who was Augustine? Who was Monica?
3. What is the Marshmallow Test? Why do we care?
4. What did Alan Kreider say led to the rapid growth of the early church?

LOVE

The Good Samaritan Revisited

> *O LORD God of heaven, the great and awesome God who keeps covenant and steadfast love with those who love him and keep his commandments.*
> (Neh 1:5)

The fourth characteristic of God in Exodus 34:6 is love. The Hebrew word *hesed*, translated as steadfast love (ESV), long-suffering (KJV), or lovingkindness (NAS) means: "obligation to the community in relation to relatives, friends, guests, master and servants; unity, solidarity, loyalty" (HOLL). Alternatively, it can be translated as "goodness, kindness." (BDAG 3279) The meaning of the Greek word used to translate hesed in the Septuagint *polueleos* is unknown.

The Greek word for love *agape* in the New Testament is the same in John and Matthew's Gospels, and means: "to have a warm regard for and interest in another, cherish, have affection for, love" (BDAG 38.1). The Hebrew word translated for agape love is: *ahabet* (Gen 22:2), not *hesed*. More generally, *agape* love is distinguished from romantic (*eros*) and brotherly (*philos*) love, because the Greek language has separate words for each. Because *agape* love and *philos* love both serve an erotic usage in the Song of Solomon (Sol 1:2–1:3), love's several definitions cause confusion.

Covenantal Love

The covenantal context of Exodus 34:6 makes it clear that the *hesed* love in view here is not a generic *agape* love, but a more specific covenantal love focused on keeping one's promises (Hafemann 2007, 33). We honor God and our neighbor by treating them with respect and keeping our word, especially when it hurts. When we marry, we assume a heartfelt relationship, but we depend on our spouses to keep their promises.

The ethical image of God is a hot-button issue today because of the proclivity of many pastors and Christians to view God exclusively through the lens of love, as we read repeatedly through the writings of the Apostle John: "Anyone who does not love does not know God, because God is love." (1 John 4:8) Matthew's double-love command is likewise frequently cited:

> Teacher, which is the great commandment in the Law? And he said to him, You shall love the Lord your God with all your heart and with all your soul and with all your mind. This is the great and first commandment. And a second is like it: You shall love your neighbor as yourself. On these two commandments depend all the Law and the Prophets. (Matt 22:36–40)

Agape love is less helpful in understanding God's character because of the wide scope in Hebrew and Greek usage and the wild definitions of love floating around in postmodern culture (e.g. Rogers 2009, 52–65). Confusion over the meaning of love was already present in the first century, which we know because the Apostle Paul devoted an entire chapter to its definition in his letter to the church at Corinth (1 Cor 13), a city infamous for prostitution. One need not define a word carefully when its usage is obvious.

In the Old Testament, God interacts with his people primarily through the giving of covenants. Hafemann (2007, 21) writes:

> God's relationship with the world and his people is not a theoretical abstraction, nor is it fundamentally a subjective experience. Rather, with salvation history as its framework, this relationship is expressed in and defined by the interrelated covenants that exist through the history of redemption.

Among the many allusions to covenant-making in the Bible, none is more detailed than the covenant with Moses.

God's Mercy Precedes His Love

Bonhoeffer (1976, 50) offers an important insight here: "No one knows God unless God reveals Himself to him. And so none knows what love is except in the self-revelation of God. Love, then, is the revelation of God."

The fact that mercy, not love, is the first characteristic of God reinforces the idea that love requires an interpretation beyond the *agape* love that so many cherish. When we say that Jesus died for our sins, we experience his love by means of (or through the instrument of) his mercy. The point that mercy is more primal in the biblical context than love is also reinforced in Jesus' Beatitudes: Mercy is listed; love is not (Matt 5:3–11). When we experience God's love through his mercy, covenant-keeping love (*hesed*), not *agape* love, is in focus.

The Good Samaritan

Jesus introduces the Parable of the Good Samaritan in response to a question posed by an attorney over how to inherit eternal life (Luke 10:25). Jesus asks the attorney to answer his own question and the attorney cites the double-love command: "You shall love the Lord your God with all your heart and with all your soul and with all your strength and with all your mind, and your neighbor as yourself." (Luke 10:27) Jesus accepts this answer, but the attorney wants to know more, asking: "Who is my neighbor?" (Luke 10:29)

This context is important because the parable specifically addresses the problem with interpreting God's love. When the Samaritan stops to attend to the wounds of the man beaten by robbers, it is an example presumably of offering love to an enemy, because the man beaten is presumed to have been a Jew and Jews hated Samaritans (Matt 5:43–46). Because the Samaritan is still likely at risk of suffering the same fate as the man beaten (and there is no presumption that the Samaritan would serve as a first-century emergency medical technician), the parable has an eschatological tinge to it—it is like the clouds part and we briefly glimpse heaven itself.

The parable is more than a simple metaphor or simile because whole groups of people are symbolized—robbers, Samaritans, priests, Levites, innkeepers—making the parable more of a short morality play. It is, in fact, a symbolic fulfillment of Jesus' core mission (Matt 15:24). So how did the it end? Jesus said:

> Which of these three, do you think, proved to be a neighbor to the man who fell among the robbers? He said, "The one who showed him mercy. (Luke 10:36-37)

Here we have an echo of the story of Cain and Abel (Gen 4) because Samaritans and Jews can be thought of as estranged brothers (1 Kgs 12). However, the parable ends not with murder but with the two brothers being reunited in love as accomplished through mercy.

∞

Almighty Father,

All glory and honor, power and dominion, truth and justice are yours, because you first loved us for while we were yet sinners, you sent Christ to die for us (Rom 5:8).

Forgive our hardened hearts, our unwillingness to love as Jesus taught.

Thank you for the many blessings of this life: Our families, our health, our work, and the many benefits of modern technology.

In the power of your Holy Spirit, open our hearts, enlighten our thoughts, strengthen our hands in your service.

In the precious name of Jesus, Amen.

∞

Questions
1. Which definition of love makes the most sense to you?
2. What is hesed love? How does it differ from agape love?
3. When did Jesus tell the Parable of the Good Samaritan?
4. Why is mercy a vehicle of experiencing the love of God?
5. Is enemy love another word for mercy?

The Two Brothers

> *A soft answer turns away wrath,*
> *but a harsh word stirs up anger.*
> (Prov 15:1)

Jesus tells the story of a man with two sons, neither of whom loved their father. The younger son came to him one day and asked for his inheritance in cash. He then took the money, left town, and began living in style in a foreign country. This reckless lifestyle did not last long and soon the young man had to get a job and he had to accept degrading work. As the son's mind began to wander, he remembered his good life at home and resolved to beg his father to take him back as a household servant. When the father saw that his son was coming, he went out to meet him and wrapped his arms around him. As the son began to apologize for his horrible behavior, his father would hear none of it. He took his son, cleaned him up, and got him some new clothes (Gen 3:21). Afterwards, he threw a party for his son. Later, when his older brother came home and discovered the party, he became jealous and started behaving badly. But his father reminded him: "Celebrate and be glad, for this your brother was dead, and is alive; he was lost, and is found." (Luke 15:32)

The Parable of the Two Brothers, often called the Parable of the Prodigal Son, shows a young man going through a series of challenges—transitions—that enabled him to see his father with new eyes and to accept his father's help. Without these challenges, he—like his older brother—would not have been able to bridge the gap between him and his father. Without his father's acceptance, he could not have returned home.

Here we see the father's love for his son as the catalyst for his son's growth and maturity, a kind of coming-of-age story. Teenagers seldom grow up and mature quickly or easily. Many today experiment with drugs, exotic sexual behavior, and falling into bad company. Those that survive often turn out to be functioning adults, but not all find their way past these temptations.

In contrast to the younger brother, the older brother remained angry and stuck. He is neither able to love his brother nor his father, a pattern that today might be described as co-dependency. We might speculate that the younger boy's absence helped the father move beyond a stricter parenting style that obviously failed to engender growth in the older brother.

Grace as Love

In the Parable of the Two Sons, the father models God's grace in two archetypes represented by the two sons. In both cases, the father offers restorative justice—grace designed to allow growth—where he might have rendered criminal justice, had the sons not been in relationship.

The love that Jesus highlights in the parable is transformative because it allows renewal of relationship and the opportunity of personal growth, reminiscent of God's request of Abraham: "Go from your country and your kindred and your father's house to the land that I will show you." (Gen 12:1) Growth in relationship is a radical departure from a traditional society that more typically values loyalty in well-defined, static relationships, not independence and growth in dynamic relationships.

In my own family, historically sons were expected to serve their fathers on the farm well into middle age. My grandfather wanted to break this tradition by attending college and studying to become a pastor. This ambition was not warmly embraced, so he followed his father into farming, a source of much resentment.

A Structural Interpretation

Craig Blomberg (2012, 197) classifies Jesus' parables by their structure, not their content. He begins with an analysis of parables, like the Parable of the Two Brothers, writing:

> Many of Jesus' parables have three main characters. Quite frequently, these include an authority figure and two contrasting subordinates. The authority

figure, usually a king or master, judges between the two subordinates, who in turn exhibit contrasting behavior. These have been called monarchic parables.

Here the authority figure is a father who has two sons. Blomberg (2012, 200–201) sees one point for each character:

1. Even as the prodigal always had the option of repenting and returning home, so also all sinners, however, wicked, may confess their sins and turn to God in contrition.
2. Even as the father went to elaborate lengths to offer reconciliation to the prodigal, so also God offers all people, however undeserving, lavish forgiveness of sins if they are willing to accept it.
3. Even as the older brother should not have begrudged his brother's reinstatement but rather rejoiced in it, so those who claim to be God's people should be glad and not mad that he extends his grace even to the most undeserving.

The extraordinary love of the father is unexpected, which hints that the parable is allegorical (Blomberg 2012, 204). Jesus' parables often display a twist that subtly deviates from first-century cultural expectation. The love offered by the father is also unconditional, contrary to Jewish tradition.

Because growing up and leaving home involves many forms of loss that must be grieved, such growth is difficult under the best of circumstances (Mitchell and Anderson 1983, 51). This makes Abraham's journey of faith and ours all the more remarkable in this time when many have turned the noun *adult* into a verb.

∞

Almighty Father,

We praise you for your modeling of unconditional love that permits us to grow and realize our potential, something especially problematic at a time when so many people die early from preventable causes.

Forgive our obstinate hearts, our distracted thoughts, and our lazy hands.

Thank you for the gift of your son, Jesus Christ, who lived a sinless life, died on the cross, and rose from the dead to atone for our sins and to offer us salvation.

In the power of your Holy Spirit, open our hearts, illumine our minds, and strengthen our hands in your service.

In Jesus' precious name, Amen.

∞

Questions
1. How can love serve as a catalyst for growth?
2. What do the two brothers share in common? How does that change?
3. What makes this coming-of-age story interesting today?

The Friend at Midnight

> *And he arose and came to his father.*
> *But while he was still a long way off,*
> *his father saw him and felt compassion,*
> *and ran and embraced him and kissed him.*
> (Luke 15:20)

One attribute of God revealed in the Parable of the Two Brothers is multiplication. When the younger son took steps to confess his sin to this father, the father took many steps to forgive him and to express his love.

This is not a *quid-pro-quo* transaction. This overwhelming generosity appears throughout scripture. It is especially seen in the Gospel of John in the quantity of wine produced at the wedding at Cana (John 2:6–10), in the bread multiplied in the feeding of the five thousand (John 6:5–14), and in the disciple's catch of fish in Galilee (John 21:4–13). God is not stingy with his love.

Seeker Love

A contemporary example of God's super-generous love arises in the context of denial of faith. In Jesus' Parable of the Two Brothers, at first neither brother loves his father. The younger brother hates his father so much he demands his inheritance while his father is still alive. The older brother practices a more insidious, passive-aggressive form of hatred: He pretends to love his father while secretly hating him, which leaves no door open to reconciliation. When the younger brother returns to his father, he opens the door to reconciliation out of his own need and shame, but only the tiniest bit—this is still not love. At best, it is a test of his father's love.

We see a similar test of God's love in Pascal's Wager. Blaise Pascal (1623–1662), a French mathematician, used probability theory to argue that the agnostic argument is logically false because faith is a fair bet where the odds favor the wager. If God exists and you believe, then you win heaven, but if God does not exist, you lose nothing. In other words, faith in God has a positive reward provided the probability of God existing is a positive, non-zero number. With faith in God, everyone is a winner.

Betting that God exists offers better odds than organized gambling, where the odds favor the house. The substantial profits earned by gambling houses and state lotteries signals a sucker's bet, not a fair bet, which is designed to prey on the poverty and ignorance of gambling addicts, who are impatient with life. Economists view lotteries as a regressive tax that targets the poor, who often believe that they have nothing left to lose. It's like the unscrupulous boss who invites construction workers for beer and a poker game on paydays knowing that when everyone sobers up, he will be holding their paychecks. Unlike all that, with faith in God, everyone is a winner.

Pascal's Wager does not engender faith, but it leads to taking faith seriously out of pecuniary benefit—the chance to win a bet. If faith is a fair bet, then the person considering Pascal's Wager has to wonder why. Taking the next step—placing the bet—is a try-before-you-buy or fake-it-until-you-make-it kind of faith commitment. In a world where faith in God is treated as philosophical nonsense and dismissed out of hand, this tiny step defines one as a seeker.

Do you think that our generous God, who is known for his overwhelming love, would ignore such a seeker? On the contrary, the Parable of the Two Brothers suggests that God will run to meet us. Elsewhere we read: "God shows his love for us in that while we were still sinners, Christ died for us." (Rom 5:8)

The Friend at Midnight

The Parable of the Two Brothers is not Jesus' only parable of extraordinary love. Consider:

> And he said to them, which of you who has a friend will go to him at midnight and say to him, Friend, lend me three loaves, for a friend of mine has arrived on a journey, and I have nothing to set before him; and he

will answer from within, do not bother me; the door is now shut, and my children are with me in bed. I cannot get up and give you anything? I tell you, though he will not get up and give him anything because he is his friend, yet because of his impudence he will rise and give him whatever he needs. (Luke 11:5-8)

What is love? Love is being willing to help a friend only because he asked, no matter how inconvenient. The word for imprudence is also translated as persistence (NAS), shameless audacity (TNIV), and importunity (KJV).

Presence as Love

Jesus uses this parable to introduce one his most famous statements: "And I tell you, ask, and it will be given to you; seek, and you will find; knock, and it will be opened to you. For everyone who asks receives, and the one who seeks finds, and to the one who knocks it will be opened." (Luke 11:5-10) The invitation to ask, seek, and knock means that with God one always has access. Access is love limited only by our unwillingness to ask for it in prayer.

An unspoken assumption here is that God is always present because otherwise how would he know that you asked? With God, we are never alone. Many times we ignore God's presence with us and undervalue the ministry of presence, which can be one of the hardest ministries to appreciate and understand. When we get over our ignorance, the ministry of presence is a priceless gift we can then extend to others.

∞

Loving Father,

All glory and honor, power and dominion, truth and justice are yours, because you first loved us and showed us what love looks like when it is most inconvenient.

Forgive us for loving the wrong things and returning love only when it is convenient, like the social climber who only loves friends who can do them a favor.

Thank you for the sacrificial love of Christ, who loved us enough to die for us even though we were unlovely, broken, and selfish, like the teenager who only wanted his father's money.

In the power of your Holy Spirit, turn our selfish hearts to you and the things that you love. May we offer a ministry of presence to those in need and turn to you in our own pain.

In Jesus' precious name and for your glory, Amen.

∞

Questions
1. What is multiplication in the context of the Parable of the Two Brothers?
2. What is Pascal's Wager?
3. How does the Parable of the Friend at Midnight extend our understanding of God's love?
4. What is a ministry of presence?

The Dragnet

> *What man of you, having a hundred sheep,*
> *if he has lost one of them,*
> *does not leave the ninety-nine in the open country,*
> *and go after the one that is lost, until he finds it?*
> (Luke 15:4)

No survey of love in the parables is complete without an examination of the Parable of the Lost Sheep. While the parable clearly exhibits God's grace, as already mentioned, it is hard to isolate this grace from *hesed* love. There is an implicit bond, a covenant of care, between a shepherd and the sheep—ownership implies care. Even a superpower recognizes an obligation to protect weaker allies, like a mother cares for her child or a duck for her ducklings.

Still, several aspects of the Parable of the Lost Sheep are unsettling in its presentation of love, starting with the word, lost. The word, lost, in the Greek *apollymi* (BDAG 958) can mean: "1. to cause or experience destruction; 2. to fail to obtain what one expects or anticipates, lose out on, lose; or 3. to lose something that one already has or be separated from a normal connection, lose, be lost." How did this sheep get lost and who is responsible? Why does the shepherd leave the other ninety-nine sheep unattended while he searches for the lost sheep? It appears that the value placed on the lost sheep is imprudent, even reckless.

When we take the next step and apply this parable to sinners, this parable becomes even more awkward. Does God love sinners more than the faithful? The righteous seem to get a bum rap in this parable. Actually, the cheeky nature of this parable is the main point: We are all sinners; none are righteous; all have fallen short of the glory of God. This parable makes no sense without the doctrine of original sin (Ps 14). The ninety-nine righteous people are an illusion—none are righteous (Luke 18:18–19). We are all lost sheep. Blomberg (2012, 216) observes that many interpret "righteous" to imply more like "self-righteous," which speaks to a problem of religious complacency. No one wants to be seen as lost.

The Dragnet

The need for vigilance among the faithful is reinforced by the many parables that focuses on judgment, like the Parable of the Dragnet. Here we read:

> Again, the kingdom of heaven is like a net that was thrown into the sea and gathered fish of every kind. When it was full, men drew it ashore and sat down and sorted the good into containers but threw away the bad. So it will be at the end of the age. The angels will come out and separate the evil from the righteous and throw them into the fiery furnace. In that place there will be weeping and gnashing of teeth. (Matt

13:47–50)

Judgment makes the point that it is hard for God honestly to love the good (righteous) if he doesn't hate the bad (evil).

This dichotomous world of good and bad fish pictured bothers most Christians today because they reject moralistic thinking. For a first-century Jew, the picture here is of righteous people who obey the Mosaic covenant and of unrighteous who do not. In the parable, the sorting of good and bad is initially done by the fishermen, who keep the good and recycle the bad. Later, these fishermen are described as angels who throw the evil into the fiery furnace without saying what becomes of the righteous.

It is helpful to recast the dichotomous picture here as our response to pain during a Gethsemane moment. When we face a painful moment or a painful choice, do we turn to God and give it over to him or do we turn into the pain and sulk? (Matt 26:39) When we habitually do one or the other, our personalities and culture are formed and hardened.

Lewis (1973, 10–11) describes hell as a place where people choose to move further and further apart. In like manner, the judgement suggested by the Parable of the Dragnet is something we impose on ourselves, not something imposed by God.

The Good News is that Christ died for our sins so we

don't have to.

∞

Almighty Father,

All glory and honor, power and dominion, truth and justice are yours, because Jesus lived a sinless life, died on the cross for our sins, and rose from the dead that we might have the hope of eternal life. In whom else shall we believe?

Forgive our besetting sins, the ones so close to our hearts that we repeat them over and over. We confess that we love our sins and can only be rid of them with your forbearance and assistance. In whom else shall we believe?

Thank you for our families, our health, our means of support, and our salvation in you. Thank you for the opportunity to minister to others and expand your holy kingdom. In whom else shall we believe?

In the power of your Holy Spirit, grant us strength to live each day, the grace to witness to those around us, and the peace that passes all understanding, your shalom. Draw us to you—open our hearts, illumine our thoughts, and strengthen our hands in your service.

In Jesus's precious name, Amen.

Questions
1. What is the covenant of care between the shepherd and the sheep?
2. What does it mean to be lost?
3. What is awkward about the Parable of the Lost Sheep?
4. How does judgment relate to love?
5. What is a Gethsemane moment and why is it special?

Applying Love

> *Know therefore that the LORD your God is God,*
> *the faithful God who keeps covenant*
> *and steadfast love with those who love him*
> *and keep his commandments, to a thousand generations,*
> *and repays to their face those who hate him,*
> *by destroying them.*
> (Deut 7:9–10)

In the parables examined, we begin to see that God's love has many facets.

Jesus introduces the Parable of the Good Samaritan to address the problem with interpreting God's love. When the Samaritan stops to attend to the wounds of the man beaten by robbers, it is an example of offering love to an enemy, because the man beaten is presumed to have been a Jew and Jews hated Samaritans (Matt 5:43–46). More than this, there is also an echo of the story of Cain and Abel (Gen 4) in the parable. Samaritans and Jews can be thought of as estranged brothers—the Northern and Southern Kingdoms of Israel—who have been reunited in love (1 Kgs 12). The parable thus pictures love allegorically as reconciliation of the long-divided, Davidic Kingdom under the umbrella of God's love.

If the Parable of the Good Samaritan shows love as a conduit to reconciliation, the Parable of the Two Brothers displays love as a catalyst for adolescent growth and maturity. This idea is reminiscent of God's request of Abraham: "Go from your country and your kindred and your father's house to the land that I will show you." (Gen 12:1).

This reality of God's love is captured in the adage: God doesn't so much care what you do as the person you become. Where we might envision a context of criminal justice, God is more interested in restorative justice which, like Jesus with the woman caught in adultery, he focused proleptically on the person she could be, not the person she had been (Campbell 2010, 11–12).

In these two parables, love is not a static description of adoration so much as a dynamic strategy for growth, reconciliation, and restoration. Furthermore, the love of the father for the prodigal son multiplies the love that the son displays. This is not a transactional love between two narcissists, but a transformative love that, like the Parable of the Friend at Midnight and enemy love, comes at a cost and is never convenient. Getting out of bed at midnight to offer hospitality to a neighbor in need is never convenient.

The reckless love of the Shepherd for the Lost Sheep is most meaningful when we realize that we are all lost sheep.

The dichotomous world of good and bad fish illustrated in the Parable of the Dragnet highlights the cost of such reckless love and serves to shock us out of complacency. Do we turn to God in our pain or sulk in our grief? Over time, Gethsemane moments move from a decision to a habit to a lifestyle that defines the person we become and the culture we engender. The reckless love of God is more than the threat of judgment that gives us a reason to turn to God in our pain.

In Christ, love is an open-handed affection with an eye on the future and the person that we become.

∞

Blessed Lord Jesus,

All glory and honor, power and dominion, truth and justice are yours, because you patiently loved us, taught us reconciliation, offered us restoration, and sheltered us as we grew to maturity.

Forgive our wandering hearts, footloose thoughts, and wanton desires. We confess that we are undeserving of your affections.

Thank you for your mercy on the cross, forgiving our sin while we were indifferent to you and those around us.

In the power of your Holy Spirit, draw us to yourself.

Open our hearts, illumine our thoughts, and strengthen our hands in your service.

In the name of the Father, the Son, and the Holy Spirit, Amen.

∞

Question
1. What is your favorite parable? Why?
2. Why does the Parable of the Good Samaritan allude to estranged brothers? Which ones?
3. How can love become a catalyst for growth and reconciliation?
4. What is the difference between static and dynamic love?

FAITH

The Rock

> *I am the way, and the truth, and the life.*
> *No one comes to the Father except through me.*
> (John 14:6)

The fifth characteristic of God in Exodus 34:6 is faithful, also translated as truthful. The Hebrew word *emuth* translates as firmness, faithfulness, truth (BDB 601). The Greek word in the Septuagint *elemon* means "to be concerned about people in their need, merciful, sympathetic, compassionate of God" (BDAG 2487). In English, we might describe someone as being true to their word, especially when it involves cost. The idea that God himself is truth pervades the biblical witness.

The Great I Am

The divine image of God lends stability to our lives that cannot be obtained any other way. When God reveals himself to Moses in the burning bush, Moses asks God his name. God responds with an enigmatic statement: "I am who I am." (Exod 3:14). In vernacular English, a paraphrase might be: I am the real deal—I exist: Deal with it.

Mathematics suggests that we should. Houston Smith (2001, 89) paraphrases Gödel's Incompleteness Theorem with this description:

> His famous Incompleteness Theorem states that in a

formal system satisfying certain precise conditions, there will always be at least one undecidable proposition—that is, a proposition such that neither it nor its negation is provable within the system (Smith 2001, 89).

God provides the one assumption from outside the universes' closed system that stabilizes the entire system. The existence of one God implies that one set of physical laws exists throughout the universe (and vice versa). Our reality is determined by God and is evident through physical law.

Known Reality

If God defines objective truth, which was the dominant value in the modern era, then postmodernism, which argues there are multiple truths (e.g. my truth, your truth), is inherently polytheistic. First-century people outside of Israel believed that the gods were territorial. We might anticipate a polytheistic world to have fundamentally different physical laws in different territories. Everywhere that scientists have studied, such differing physical laws are nowhere present.

The implications of Gödel's Incompleteness Theorem are far-reaching. In psychology, for example, we observe that faith in God serves to stabilize our psyches. The prevalence of anxiety and depression in the postmodern period may simply be a barometer of the falling away from faith in this generation.

The Rock

This problem of being out of sync with reality is, in fact, an important takeaway from the Parable of the Two Builders found in Matthew and Luke:

> Everyone who comes to me and hears my words and does them, I will show you what he is like: he is like a man building a house, who dug deep and laid the foundation on the rock. And when a flood arose, the stream broke against that house and could not shake it, because it had been well built. But the one who hears and does not do them is like a man who built a house on the ground without a foundation. When the stream broke against it, immediately it fell, and the ruin of that house was great. (Luke 6:47–49)

Instead of focusing on the builders here, consider the rock. The builders can either utilize the rock to guarantee stability or save a few bucks by not. The reality of the rock does not change whether they do or do not build on it.

The rock is an apt analogy today where we see videos every day of coastal property being eroded by rising sea levels and apartment buildings crashing into heaps of dust shaken by earthquakes. How are builders today to respond to these obvious ecological challenges?

Allegorical Truth

Jesus does not, however, tell the Parable of the Two Builders to provide construction advice; it is a simile, as the first sentence makes explicit: "Everyone who comes to me and hears my words and does them, I will show you what he is like. …" (Luke 6:47). The question in view here is about truth. The need to build with a foundation is a concrete, practical truth that parallels the spiritual truth of God.

The argument here is from the lesser to the greater, which is necessary because a transcendent entity is unobservable. A postmodern example of transcendence might be cell-phone technology, whose function is unobserved by users not trained in computer programming and solid-state engineering. The cell phone accordingly operates through processes that transcend daily experience.

Faith in God is accordingly counter-cultural and has the benefit of preparing our minds for other transcendent concepts, like mathematics and science, in at least two ways. First, knowing that God created the universe (and is a God of truth), we expect it to be orderly and worthy of scientific study. Second, a disciplined lifestyle and allegorical thinking in one realm makes it easier to apply the same talents in another field of inquiry, such as science. A materialistic, polytheist would harbor no such predilections and, as a consequence, would be less likely than people of faith to populate the scientific community.

∞

Spirit of Truth,

All honor and glory, power and dominion, truth and justice are yours, because you lay the foundations of the earth and heaven, sustain all things, and show us how to honor beauty, truth, and justice.

Forgive us for our neglect of your creation, the people around us, and your church.

Thank you for the gift of the scriptures, your presence, and the many blessings of this life.

In the power of your presence, teach us your ways that we might share them with the people around us. Be our rock in the midst of the storm.

In Jesus' precious name, Amen.

∞

Questions
1. How does God manifest truth?
2. What is the source of stability in our lives and our world?
3. Why is postmodern society inherently polytheistic?
4. In what two ways is faith conducive to science and technology?
5. What is allegory?

The Callous Judge

> *Pilate said to him, What is truth?*
> (John 18:38)

Truth comes in many forms, some of which we prefer to ignore. The Book of Job articulates three ethical systems that are often in conflict:

1. One is good if one obeys the law (law).
2. One is smart when one understands how the world really works (wisdom).
3. One can only be justified through divine intervention (grace).

What then is truth? Pilate was smart enough to ask the question, but did not have the courage to act on what he knew.

The Parable of the Callous Judge

Sometimes leaders do the right thing for the wrong reason, as Jesus illustrates in the Parable of the Callous Judge:

> And he told them a parable to the effect that they ought always to pray and not lose heart. He said, In a certain city there was a judge who neither feared God nor respected man. And there was a widow in that city who kept coming to him and saying, Give me justice against my adversary. For a while he refused, but afterward he said to himself, Though I neither fear God nor respect man, yet because this widow keeps bothering me, I will give her justice, so that she will not beat me down by her continual coming. And the Lord said, hear what the unrighteous judge says. And will

not God give justice to his elect, who cry to him day and night? Will he delay long over them? I tell you, he will give justice to them speedily. Nevertheless, when the Son of Man comes, will he find faith on earth? (Luke 18:1–8)

It is interesting that Jesus relates this story of conflicting motivations with faith. Too often we find ourselves struggling with multiple motivations. In the parable, the judge acts on behalf of the widow, not because it is the right thing to do under the law, but because he wants to stop her nagging. It is to his own benefit, not hers, which prompts him to act.

The Ethical Dilemma

Motivations and even principles often come in tension with one another. Bonhoeffer (1976, 367) cites this example:

> A teacher asks a child in front of the class whether it is true that his father often comes home drunk. It is true, but the child denies it. The teacher's question has placed him in a situation for which he is not yet prepared. He feels only that what is taking place is an unjustified interference in the order of the family and that he must oppose it.

In Bonhoeffer's example, the student is presented with an ethical dilemma and must choose between the commandments to tell the truth (Exod 20:16) and to honor your parents (Exod 20:12). How do you decide which commandment is more important?

More generally, the Ten Commandments provide

theological principles outlining good and bad behavior. It is helpful to distinguish good and bad principles from right and wrong actions (Johnson and Zerbi 1973, 12). In Bonhoeffer's example, it is good for the student to tell the truth and to honor his parents, but it is wrong for the teacher to pose the question about the father's drunken behavior (and embarrass the student publicly) and wrong for the student to verify it in public.

Principal Agent Problem

The Parable of the Callous Judge and the Bonhoeffer story are both examples of a principal agent problem, which arises when a leader makes organizational decisions based on personal benefits rather than organizational benefits. In the Bonhoeffer example, suppose that the teacher is a sadist who derives pleasure from tormenting students. By putting the student on the spot to verify the father's drunkenness in public, the teacher derives sadistic pleasure at the risk of opening the school up to a potential lawsuit from the student's family. In doing so, the teacher's interests and the school interests deviate demonstrating the principal agent problem.

Sexual harassment, pedophilia, taking bribes, and narcissistic leadership are all potential manifestations of the principal agent problem. In the postmodern context, a distinguishing characteristic of an amoral organization is that leadership prosecutes principal agent problems while generally eschewing the moral failings of members and leaders.

In a world of conflicting motivation and incomplete information, law and worldly wisdom are insufficient. The intervention of the Holy Spirit remains our only option. In the Parable of the Callous Judge, we meet a God who desires to be part of our daily lives.

∞

Almighty Father,

All praise and honor, power and dominion, truth and justice are yours, because you teach us to the honor the law, be mindful of the world, and advise us when wisdom and knowledge fail us.

We confess that you alone are the Lord. Nothing happens without your permission, but we are rude, impertinent, and too quick to judge others. Forgive our hardened hearts and willful minds.

We give thanks that you are willing to overlook our shortcomings, teach us, and lead us where we need to go.

In the power of your Holy Spirit, quicken our consciouses that we might not sin. Remind us of your law, teach us about the ways of the world, and guide us even when we too easily stray.

In Jesus's precious name, Amen.

∞

Questions
1. What are the three ethical systems found in the Book of Job?
2. What is a principal agent problem, and why do we care?
3. What is the lesson of the Parable of the Callous Judge?
4. What does it mean to have multiple motivations?
5. What is an ethical dilemma?

Pharisee and Tax Collector

> *In the beginning,*
> *God created the heavens and the earth.*
> (Gen 1:1)

Two words of theological importance in understanding God are transcendent and immanent. To say that God is transcendent means that he stands above or outside of the universe that he created. Normally we attribute transcendence to God the Father because of his role in creation. Just like a carpenter is not part of a cabinet that he builds, God stands outside the universe because he created it. By contrast, when we call Jesus Emmanuel—God with us, as the name means in Hebrew—we are highlighting his immanence.

Have you ever wondered how God hears our prayers? If God the Father is transcendent and Jesus is immanent, just not standing in front of us, how does God know what we are praying, especially when we do not mouth the words? I have always seen this as a role of the Holy Spirit, God within us. The Holy Spirit is the power of God that sustains and provisions us, grants us spiritual gifts, and hears our prayers. As we read: "And the Spirit of God was hovering over the face of the waters." (Gen 1:2) Hovering requires time and energy, just like your telephone requires electricity.

The Parable of the Pharisee and the Tax Collector

The Parable of the Pharisee and the Tax Collector, discussed earlier, pictures two worshippers in the temple praying. God the Father is normally considered the object of their prayer, but this parable includes an observer, Jesus Christ, who interprets the parable for us. It is Christ himself who cautions us: "For everyone who exalts himself will be humbled, but the one who humbles himself will be exalted." (Luke 18:14)

The sort of humility in view in this parable is that of self-reflection. A self-reflective person is one who is open to learning from their own experience. I used to tell my kids that there are three kinds of people in this world: Those who never learn, those who learn from their own mistakes, and those who learn from other people's mistakes. While the parable appears to focus on this second type of learner, it is generally true that people who pray are open to learning from God, which implies that Jesus does not discount the third type of learner.

More generally in this parable, we witness God's attribute of accessibility. God is accessible in prayer (through the Holy Spirit) and he is accessible through Jesus Christ by means of his parables. This accessibility is not constrained by the manner of prayer, but it is better to be humble than self-praising if you want to be justified. Here in this parable we see a God who stands as judge over both our actions and our prayers.

Justification Before God

The Greek key term in this parable dikaio means: *To take up a legal cause, show justice, do justice, take up a cause.* (BDAG 2005). Justify is a legal term as used in Luke 18:14. The idea here is that a self-reflective, humble person is more likely to be right with God than someone full of themselves.

More normally, we eschew a strictly legal interpretation of our relationship with God and prefer being called children of God, which suggests a more intimate relationship. But children can be either obedient or disobedient. Perhaps, a better way to look at it is to say we relate to God on multiple levels, depending on circumstances. The Good News is that regardless of circumstances, we are still members of God's family.

∞

Blessed Lord Jesus,

All praise and honor, power and dominion, truth and justice are yours because you are always available and hear our prayers.

We confess that we are not always fully present to those around us. Our minds wander and we wander through life without purpose or honor.

Thank you for the many blessings of this life, those that are obvious and those that we only discover as time passes.

In the power of your Holy Spirit, create in us a clean heart and a right spirit that we might be fully present and share your presence with those around us.

In the name of the Father, the Son, and the Holy Spirit, Amen.

∞

Questions
1. What is the difference between transcendence and immanence?
2. How does God answer your prayers?
3. What does humility mean to you?
4. What does it mean to be available?
5. Do you feel justified before God? How and why?

The Physician

> *This shall be the law of the leprous person*
> *for the day of his cleansing.*
> *He shall be brought to the priest.*
> (Lev 14:2)

The nature of truth and faithfulness takes on a whole new level of significance when lives are at stake. Although one can pray about most anything, our minds often fixate on medical situations when someone asks if anyone is in need of prayer. When it comes to medical conditions, we feel vulnerable, alone, and, many times, hopeless.

The Great Physician

Jesus is best known as a healer both of body and spirit. Even Jesus' most adamant critics admit that he was an exorcist, which seems odd because in the next breath these same critics will deny the existence of demons that can be exorcised (Sanders 1993, 15). How can Jesus exorcise demons that don't exist? Even more odd, in this materialistic world where people deny the existence of God, these same materialists seem obsessed with the demonic, if Hollywood movies be any guide to public perceptions. The existence of the spiritual world appears to reveal a cleavage between thoughts and feelings of many people.

Roman Catholic priest Francis MacNutt noted four types

of healing prayer:

1. Repentance of sin (spiritual healing),
2. Emotional (or relational) healing,
3. Physical healing, and
4. Deliverance (healing from spiritual oppression) (MacNutt 2009, 130).

In the New Testament, we see Jesus healing people in each of these categories. Jesus could easily be described as the first medical missionary.

Spiritual Connection to Ailments

We live in a time when the spiritual relationship to medical problems is most obvious because the leading causes of death are preventable. Preventable illnesses and conditions point to a spiritual problem because the only things standing between the condition and treatment is a decision. Suicide, drug overdoses, obesity, and refusing to be vaccinated are leading causes of death in America today—so much so that life expectancy has been declining in recent years.

There is no shame in visiting a doctor in this materialistic world, but don't tell me I need to see a pastor or priest—I am not crazy—people tell themselves. Interestingly, Carl Jung (1955, 31), a student of Sigmund Freud, described the psychiatrist as a priest in a secular religion. Counseling in this framework serves as the confessional in this new religion where the patient confesses his sins and the counselor then proscribes the steps to be taken to receive absolution. Jung supported this interpretation of Freud's psychiatry noting Freud's use of numerous speculative myths to support his theories, such as his theory of penis envy.

Parable of the Physician

One of Jesus' shortest parables appears to be nothing more than a declarative sentence: "Those who are well have no need of a physician, but those who are sick." (Matt 9:12). This parable is one of Jesus' proverbs, which in Hebrew is one type of parable. The same sentence appears in Matthew, Mark, and Luke, albeit in different contexts.

The sentence appears as a doublet in Mark: "Those who are well have no need of a physician, but those who are sick. I came not to call the righteous, but sinners." (Mark 2:17) A Hebrew doublet is a poetic expression where the primary statement is repeated in different words in the second. Thus, Jesus is equating sin to sickness. This parallel is interesting because the Apostle Paul famously said: "For the wages of sin is death." (Rom 6:23) If sin is the cause of illness and death, then physicians are effectively called upon to treat our sin, just like pastors and priests.

The Matthew version of this parable inserts a phrase not found in Mark or Luke: "Go and learn what this means: I desire mercy, and not sacrifice." (Matt 9:13) Mercy is one of the Beatitudes in Matthew 5 and it is the first attribute of God mentioned in Exodus 34:6.

∞

Great Physician,

All praise and glory, power and dominion, truth and justice are yours, because you heal our diseases without appointment or cost. You only ask that we have faith.

We confess that faith is hard for us. We want your gifts without commitment, without thought, without devoting our hearts to what our eyes see every day. Forgive our materialistic attitudes and unrighteous living.

Thank you for the gift of forgiveness that Jesus made possible on the cross. Thank you for the many Easter eggs, blessings that you have given us with science, like the treats that we hide where we know our kids will find them.

In the power of your Holy Spirit, turn our eyes to you that our hearts will follow. Heal our sin-sick lives that our bodies and minds might also be healed.

In Jesus's precious name, Amen.

Questions
1. What is the most common focus of prayer?
2. Why is a materialist worldview at odds with our spiritual well-being?
3. What are four types of healing?
4. How do medical problems connect to our spiritual condition?

Applying Faith

> *Now faith is the assurance of things hoped for,*
> *the conviction of things not seen.*
> (Heb 11:1)

In the parables examined, we begin to see the nature of God's faithfulness and truth. The fifth characteristic of God in Exodus 34:6 is faithful, also translated as truthful. Often in scripture, the faithfulness and truthfulness of God is assumed, not described, which is also true of the parables.

Parables of Truth and Faithfulness

The divine image of God lends stability to our lives that cannot be obtained any other way. In the Parable of the Two Builders, God is the rock on which our foundations are made secure. The rock of our salvation is a metaphor both for a disciplined lifestyle and for scientific study. Allegorically, it is also a symbol of faith. Without that rock, neither fruit of such stability is possible.

In the Parable of the Callous Judge, we are advised to study the wisdom of the world. Knowledge of the world is part of God's truth. Paying attention to the principal agent problem, recognizing what motivates even evil people, may offend our sensibilities, but should not be neglected as we faithfully attend to our role as stewards of our time, resources, and persons under our care.

The Parable of the Pharisee and the Tax Collector reminds us that God is both transcendent (the object of our prayers) and immanent (able to hear our prayers). Even though God is beyond our comprehension, he loves us enough to remain always available. Whether we are faithful or naughty, we remain through faith part of God's family.

The Parable of the Physician takes the form of a proverb and simply describes the role of a doctor in healing the sick. It is a brilliant statement of the obvious: Simple proverb; profound truth. Yet doctors more often attend to the whims of the rich than to illnesses of those poor and sick. Furthermore, Jesus uses this proverb allegorically to describe his role as a rabbi and medical missionary.

Here we see Jesus highlighting the principal agent problem that afflicts religious leaders. As with the physician that serves as a personal doctor of the wealthy, religious leaders often spend more time with paying customers than with those in need of their care. This problem likely describes Jesus' impatience and distain for religion leaders, but it is equally true of today's counselors and psychologists. The Parable of the Physician is one of Jesus's more poignant parables and, because of its brevity, one of the most neglected among commentators.

Problem of Truth

More than other attributes of God described in Exodus 34:6, examples of parables directed specifically at truthfulness and faithfulness are hard to find. More often we observe lessons about truth and faith from the context and structure of the parables. Pilate's question—What is Truth?—is not simply a throw-away comment (John 18:38). When we say that God is truth, we recognize the enigma at the heart of the concept.

∞

God of all wonders and truth,

All praise and honor, power and dominion, truth and justice are yours, because you honor truth and faithfully make yourself available to us in our hour of need.

We confess that we are more likely distracted when we should be available. Even when we don the cloth and take on a doctor's scrubs, we have trouble being fully present to those in need whom we presumably serve. Forgive us.

Thank you for the example of Jesus of Nazareth and the presence of the Holy Spirit who give direction and grant us hope that we can more faithfully discharge our duties as Christians in a fallen world and truly witness to those around us.

In the power of your Holy Spirit, enable us to utilize the gifts that you have given us.

In Jesus' precious name, Amen.

∞

Questions
1. Which parables speak to you most clearly of God's faithfulness and truth?
2. What is special about the context and structure of Jesus' parables?
3. What is the meaning of the rock of our salvation?
4. Why is the Parable of the Physician particularly significant?

CONCLUSION

Who God is Not

Teacher, tell my brother to divide the inheritance with me. But he said to him, Man, who made me a judge or arbitrator over you?

(Luke 12:13–14)

The parables do not always tell us what we want to hear or explain things plainly. They draw us in and force us to confront our own motivations and relationships, particularly with God, through stories about our own lives. They also provide information about who God is not.

Things not descriptive of God arise directly from his characteristics. A merciful God is not capricious. A gracious God does not pic nits the way that Satan slanders, taunts, and tricks us. God is not impatient, unloving, or unfaithful. These observations are obvious, but it is helpful to review them because of the many distortions floating around.

When people try to twist the image of God for their own purposes, we need to discern what is being done. Not everyone reads their Bible carefully and with good intentions. In the Garden of Eden, Satan twists God's words in tempting Eve: "Did God actually say, You shall not eat of any tree in the garden?" (Gen 3:1) Again, when Satan tempts Jesus in the desert, he misquotes scripture three times and Jesus corrects him (Luke 4:3–13). We should not be surprised when this happens in our own lives.

Brothers in Conflict

In Luke 12, Jesus is put on the spot by two brothers arguing over their inheritance. We are not told the details of the dispute, but as anyone who has had to deal with inheritance issues can tell you, such disputes are often animated and painful. Who gets what and how much strikes deep into the quality of relationships with parents and siblings at a time when grief is still fresh. Such disputes can tear families apart and divide them for decades.

Jesus wisely refuses to be drawn into the brother's dispute, not wanting to enable conflict. The Book of Genesis recounts a number of brotherly disputes, like the jealousy of Cain over his brother Abel's better relationship with God (Gen 4:3–8). In the cases of Isaac and Ishmael (Gen 21:10), Jacob and Essau (Gen 25:29–34), and Joseph and his brothers (Gen 37:3), the family disputes revolved specifically around birthrights, inheritance, and leadership succession. The division of the Nation of Israel into the Northern and Southern Kingdoms, often pictured as feuding brothers, occurred after Solomon died and his son, Rehoboam, succeeded him and he was asked to lower taxes (1 Kgs 12). Taxes, like inheritance, is a money question.

Parable of the Rich Man

In response to the two brothers quarreling over their inheritance, Jesus tells a story:

> The land of a rich man produced plentifully, and he thought to himself, What shall I do, for I have nowhere to store my crops? And he said, I will do this: I will tear down my barns and build larger ones, and there I will store all my grain and my goods. And I will say to my soul, Soul, you have ample goods laid up for many years; relax, eat, drink, be merry. But God said to him, Fool! This night your soul is required of you, and the things you have prepared, whose will they be? So is the one who lays up treasure for himself and is not rich toward God. (Luke 12:16–21)

This parable could easily describe the usual series of events leading up to retirement. The problem is that retirement is not a Christian concept—we just get more opportunity to choose how we spend our time. In my case, I hope to spend more time with my grandchildren than I had to spend with my kids.

The parable of the rich man echoes Ecclesiastes: "And I commend joy, for man has nothing better under the sun but to eat and drink and be joyful, for this will go with him in his toil through the days of his life that God has given him under the sun." (Eccl 8:15) It is, however, one thing to practice Sabbath rest, it is another thing to eschew God and enjoy a life of ease (Heb 4).

In a world where children starve, sloth is an abomination

and wealth carries responsibility.

God is not an Enabler

It is ironic that Jesus refuses to judge between the two brothers, because we believe that Christ will one day judge us all (Rev 21:27). By refusing to serve as a judge between the two brothers, Jesus refuses to enable their greedy behavior. If we think about this decision allegorically, God does not want to enable conflict, whether it is between brothers, sports teams, or countries.

When the people of Israel left Egypt, out of fear they refused to trust God and enter the Promised Land. God then cursed them to remain in the desert another forty years—long enough that all who were disobedient had died.

God provides Sabbath rest, but does not enable disobedience (Heb 4). God is like good parents who educate and vacation with their kids, but does not bail them out when they misbehave and get into trouble. God is not an enabler.

∞

Lord of the Sabbath,

All praise and glory, power and dominion, truth and justice are yours, because you care for us in ways that we would never ask, yet cannot live without.

Forgive our sloth, our unwillingness to share, our greed and arrogance. Give us happy, open-handed attitudes to stem our weaknesses and pride.

Thank you for the parables of Jesus that teach us about yourself that we might grow more like you day-by-day.

In the power of your Holy Spirit, lead us through all stages of life with equal joy and faithfulness.

In Jesus' precious name, Amen.

∞

Questions
1. What are God's attributes? What is God not like?
2. Why does Jesus refuse to arbitrate between the two brothers?
3. What biblical examples can you give of brothers in conflict?
4. In you opinion, what does the Parable of the Rich Man teach?
5. What is an enabler?

Image of God

> *Ask, and it will be given to you; seek, and you will find;*
> *knock, and it will be opened to you.*
> *For everyone who asks receives, and the one who seeks finds,*
> *and to the one who knocks it will be opened.*
> (Luke 11:9–10)

What is the image of God pictured in Jesus' parables? While the Bible makes clear that God is not stingy with his love, love is not his only characteristic. God revealed himself to Moses as: "A God merciful and gracious, slow to anger, and abounding in steadfast love and faithfulness." (Exod 34:6) These five characteristics could be compared mathematically to a five-dimensional figure, not limited to the four dimensions—height, width, depth, and time—that describe the universe we inhabit.

God's transcendence works like this fifth dimension, and it is more complex than many envision. God inhabits a dimension beyond ours that opens us to see the world with new eyes. For this reason, we can never fully comprehend God, but he invites us to try. When we do, the forms that lead us to him, like the parables and worship, no longer constrain us. They simply launch us into this new dimension available only through faith.

Mercy

The nature of God's mercy is clarified in several parables.

In the Good Samaritan, we learn that mercy requires a visceral reaction: Our hearts lean into mercy more than our heads. God is emotionally involved in our lives and our salvation. In the Unforgiving Servant, we find that our forgiveness comes with the obligation to extend mercy to those who sin against us.

In the Barren Fig Tree, we learn that God's patience has limits. A good heart needs to be cultivated. Such cultivation takes a lifetime, so it should not be delayed. In the Pharisee and the Tax Collector, we find a sovereign God who favors humble believers.

While the Hebrew word for mercy is only used to describe God, Jesus' parables describe God's characteristic within a human context.

Grace

The nature of God's grace is displayed in several parables.

While God's grace is an undeserved blessing, Jesus' parable of the Hidden Treasure suggests that our response to grace is important (Matt 13:44). A gracious blessing is of little use if we hide it away and make no use of it.

Responding to God's grace is important in understanding

the Parable of the Lost Sheep. Lost sheep are more likely to be found if they listen for the shepherd's voice.

In the Parable of the Doctor and the Sick, Jesus graciously treats sin as an illness (Luke 5:31–32). This re-imaging of sin removes sin's guilt, shame, and curse to heal our hearts and our relationships.

The Parable of Lazarus and the Rich Man in Luke 16 displays grace in life and in the afterlife. The fault of the rich man is that he failed to give thanks to God for his blessings in this life and fails then to prepare for the afterlife.

In each of these parables God uses grace strategically to encourage, lead, and grow us in the context of relationship, as in the Parable of the Two Sons (Luke 15:11–32).

Patience

The importance of God's patience is obvious from several parables.

In the Parable of the Two Builders, we find patience associated with good planning and expert workmanship. Likewise, in the Parable of the Sower, we see that farming requires patient planning and a willingness to invest time and effort in a crop that is hidden from the outset.

In the Parable of the Talents, we learn to take risks to

advance the Kingdom of God while we wait patiently for the Lord's return. In the Parable of the Ten Virgins, we again see the need to plan patiently for every contingency.

The importance of patience and planning for the future in the faith suggests why Christians have always valued and invested more in education than other groups.

Love

God's love has many facets that are the focus of several parables.

Jesus introduces the Parable of the Good Samaritan as an example of offering love to an enemy (Matt 5:43–46). The parable pictures love allegorically as reconciliation of the long-divided, Davidic Kingdom under the umbrella of God's love.

If the Parable of the Good Samaritan shows love as a conduit to reconciliation, the Parable of the Two Brothers displays love as a catalyst for adolescent growth and maturity. This is a context reminiscent of God's request of Abraham: "Go from your country and your kindred and your father's house to the land that I will show you." (Gen 12:1).

In these two parables, love is not a static description of adoration so much as a dynamic strategy for growth, reconciliation, and restoration.

The reckless love of the Shepherd for the Lost Sheep is most meaningful when we realize that we are all lost sheep. The fish illustrated in the Parable of the Dragnet highlights the cost of such reckless love and serves to shock us out of complacency.

In Christ, love is an open-handed affection with an eye on the future.

Faith

The divine image of God lends stability to our lives that cannot be obtained any other way. In the Parable of the Two Builders, God is the rock on which our foundations are made secure. The rock of our salvation is a metaphor both for a disciplined lifestyle and for scientific study. In the Parable of the Callous Judge, we are advised to study the wisdom of the world.

The Parable of the Pharisee and the Tax Collector reminds us that God is both transcendent (the object of our prayers) and immanent (able to hear our prayers). Even though God is beyond our comprehension, he loves us enough to always remain available.

The Parable of the Physician takes the form of a proverb and simply describes the role of a doctor in healing the sick.

Seekers Find

Jesus' parables reveal a God who is intentionally available

to those who seek him. The parables invite the listener to enter the narrative and engage with God one-on-one to expand our understanding of faith. My Old Testament professor, who studied poetry, described scripture generally as laconic, offering descriptions with a bare number of words (Niehaus 2019, 97).

Laconic stories trigger our imaginations as we fill in missing details with our own experiences, like the husband and wife who constantly complete each other's sentences. The parables work this laconic magic better than any other part of scripture, pointing us to our transcendent God in new ways with each additional reading. Still, it comes as no surprise that we cannot easily summarize God's characteristics with any one parable or synthesis of several.

∞

Almighty and Sovereign Lord,

All praise and honor, power and dominion, truth and justice are yours, because you share all aspects of your character with us and lead us to reflect them.

Forgive us when we obsess on one attribute of your character and neglect the others in the attempt to mold you in our image when we should model yours.

Thank you for not giving up on us in our weaknesses and

sin.

In the power of your Holy Spirit, grant us the strength to reflect your image more closely, the grace to extend your image to others, and the peace that passes all understanding.

In Jesus' precious name, Amen.

∞

Questions
1. Why is Exodus 34:6 helpful in understanding Jesus' parables?
2. What is your favorite parable and why?
3. Why is God's character so complex?
4. What does laconic mean? Why is it helpful in thinking about the parables?

REFERENCES

Bauer, Walter (BDAG)[1]. 2000. *A Greek-English Lexicon of the New Testament and Other Early Christian Literature.* 3rd ed. Frederick W. Danker. Chicago: University of Chicago Press. <BibleWorks. v .9.>.

BibleWorks. 2015. Norfolk, VA: BibleWorks, LLC. <BibleWorks v.10>.

Blomberg, Craig L. 2012. *Interpreting the Parables.* Downers Grove: IVP Academic.

Bonhoeffer, Dietrich. 1976. *Ethics* (Orig Pub 1955) Edited by Eberhard Bethge. Translated by Neville Horton Smith. New York: MacMillan Publishers Company, Inc.

Bonhoeffer, Dietrich. 1995. *The Cost of Discipleship* (Orig Pub 1937). Translated by R. H. Fuller and Irmgard Booth. New York: Simon & Schuster—A Touchstone Book.

Brown-Driver-Briggs-Gesenius (BDB)[2]. 1905. *Hebrew-English Lexicon,* unabridged.

Campbell, William P. 2010. *Turning Controversy into Church Ministry: A Christlike Response to Homosexuality.* Grand Rapids: Zondervan.

---

[1] My references to BDAG are taken from the software product BibleWorks, version 10.
[2] My references to BDB are taken from the software product BibleWorks, version 10.

Dayton, Donald W. 2005. *Discovering An Evangelical Heritage* (Orig. Pub. 1976). Peabody: Hendrickson.

Dikkers, Scott. 2018. *How to Write Funny: Your Serious Step-by-Step Blueprint for Creating Incredibly, Irresistibly Successful Hilarious Writing.* Book 1. https://HowToWriteFunny.com.

Elliott, Matthew A. 2006. *Faithful Feelings: Rethinking Emotion in the New Testament.* Grand Rapids: Kregel Academic and Professional.

Enns, Gaylord. 2022. *Love Revolution: Rediscovering the Lost Command of Jesus.* Chico, CA: Love Revolution Press.

Ferguson, Sinclair B. 1996. *The Holy Spirit.* Downers Grove: InverVarsity Press.

Finney, Charles. 1999. *The Spirit-Filled Life* (Orig pub 1845–1861). New Kensington, PA: Whitaker House.

Foley, Michael P. [editor] 2006. *Augustine Confessions* (Orig Pub 397 AD). 2nd Edition. Translated by F. J. Sheed (1942). Indianapolis: Hackett Publishing Company, Inc.

Galli, Mark and Ted Olsen. 2000. *131 Christians Everyone Should Know.* Nashville: Broadman & Holman Publishers.

Georges, Jayson. 2017. *The 3-D Gospel: Ministry in Guilt, Shame, and Fear Cultures.* Time Press.

Hafemann, Scott J. 2007. "The Covenant Relationship." pp 20–65 of *Central Themes in Biblical Theology: Mapping Unity in Diversity*. Edited by Scott J. Hafemann and Paul R. House. Grand Rapids: Baker Academic.

Hart, David Bentley. 2009. *Atheist Delusions: The Christian Revolution and Its Fashionable Enemies*. New Haven: Yale University Press.

Holladay, W. L. [ed] (HOLL). 1997. *A Concise Hebrew and Aramaic Lexicon of the Old Testament*. Based upon the Lexical Work of Ludwig Koehler and Walter Baumgartner. Boston: Brill Academic Publishers.

Howard, Evan B. 2018. *A Guide to Christian Spiritual Formation: How Scripture, Spirit, Community, and Mission Shape Our Souls*. Grand Rapids: Baker Academic.

Johnson, Glenn L. and Lewis K. Zerby. 1973. *What Economists Do About Values: Case Studies of Their Answers to Questions They Don't Dare Ask*. East Lansing: Michigan State University.

Jung, Carl G. 1955. *Modern Man in Search of a Soul* (Orig Pub 1933). Translated by W.S. Dell and Cary F. Baynes. New York: Harcourt, Inc.

Keener, Craig S. 2009. *The Gospel of Matthew: A Socio-Rhetorical Commentary.* Grand Rapids: Eerdmans.

Kissenger, Warren S. 1979. *The Parables of Jesus: A History of Interpretation and Bibliography.* Metuchen, NJ: Scarcrow Press, Inc. and American Theological Library Association.

Kreeft, Peter. 2007. *The Philosophy of Jesus.* South Bend, IN: Saint Augustine Press.

Kreider, Alan. 2016. *The Patient Ferment of the Early Church.* Grand Rapids: Baker Academic.

Ladd, George Eldon. 1991. *A Theology of the New Testament* (Orig pub 1974). Grand Rapids: Eerdmans

Lewis, C.S. 1973. *The Great Divorce: A Dream.* (Orig Pub 1946). New York: HarperOne.

Longfield, Bradley J. 1991. *The Presbyterian Controversy: Fundamentalists, Modernists, and Moderates.* New York: Oxford University Press.

MacNutt, Francis. 2009. *Healing* (Orig Pub 1974). Notre Dame: Ave Maria Press.

McDonald, Suzanne. 2010. *Re-Imaging Election: Divine Election as Representing God to Others & Others to God.* Grand Rapids: Eerdmans.

Metaxas, Eric. 2014. *Miracles: What They Are, Why They Happen, and How They Can Change Your Life.* New York: Dutton.

Mischel, Walter. 2014. *The Marshmallow Test: Measuring Self-Control.* New York: Little, Brown, and Company.

Mitchell, Kenneth R. and Herbert Anderson. 1983. *All Our Losses; All Our Griefs: Resources for Pastoral Care.* Louisville: Westminster John Knox Press.

Niehaus, Jeffrey J. 2019. *God the Poet: Exploring the Origins and Nature of Poetry.* (Kindle) Bellingham, WA: Lexham Press.

Placher, William C. 1989. *Unapologetic Theology: A Christian Voice in a Pluralistic Conversation.* Louisville: Westminster John Knox Press.

Plantinga, Alvin. 2000. *Warranted Christian Belief.* New York: Oxford University Press.

Rogers, Jack. 2009. *Jesus, The Bible, and Homosexuality: Explode the Myths, Heal the Church.* Louisville: Westminster John Knox Press.

Sanders, E.P. 1993. *The Historical Figure of Jesus.* New York: Penguin Books.

Schlossberg, Herbert. 1990. *Idols for Destruction: The Conflict of Christian Faith and American Culture.* Wheaton: Crossway Books.

Smith, Houston. 2001. *Why Religion Matters: The Fate of the Human Spirit in an Age of Disbelief.* San Francisco: Harper.

Yancy, Philip. 1997. *What's So Amazing about Grace?* Grand Rapids: Zondervan.

SCRIPTURAL INDEX

OLD TESTAMENT

Genesis
1...85
1:1.......................................150
1:2.......................................150
1:3–4....................................35
1:27................................xi, 35
3:1.......................................165
3:6..44
3:21.....................................117
4...................................115, 132
4:3–8...................................166
4:6–7....................................41
4:15......................................42
7..85
9:6..42
12:1....................119, 133, 173
18:17–18...............................50
18:23....................................50
19:1......................................83
21:10...................................166
22:2.....................................111
25:29–34.............................166
37:3.....................................166

Exodus
3:14.....................................139
4:21......................................16
20..98
20:12...................................146
20:16...................................146
22:22....................................58
34:6............ix, 5, 16, 17, 27, 31, 36, 83, 87, 111, 139, 159, 170, 176
34:7......................................44
34:29......................................6

Leviticus
14:2.....................................154

Numbers
12:6–8...................................99
20:12....................................14

Deuteronomy
6:4–9......................................x
7:9–10..................................132
21:20–21................................75
28..................................73, 98

2 Samuel
7..98
12:1–7...................................13
12:7......................................13

1 Kings
12....................115, 132, 166
17..58

Nehemiah
1:5.......................................111

Psalms
14..................................46, 128
23..4
23:1..3
78..14
78:2......................................14
86:15.....................................xi
90:12....................................92

Proverbs
1:7..................................19, 83
14:29....................................83
15:1.....................................117
19:21....................................16

Eccl
8:15.....................................167

Song of Solomon
1:2–1:3 111

Isaiah
36:1 .... 36, 51

Jeremiah
31:29–30 44

Ezekiel
17 14
17:2 14
24 14
34 4
34:5–6 4

Joel
2:13 xi

Jonah
1:1–2 51
1:2 36
3:10 36
3:10 52
4:1 .... 36, 52
4:2 .... xii, 36

NEW TESTAMENT
Matthew
3:8 .... 39, 41
5:3–11 114
5:7 .... 31, 49
5:43–46 .... 114, 132, 173
6:14–15 33
9:5 68
9:12–13 68
12–13 .... xi, 9
13:3–9 88
13:3–23 88
13:13 5
13:19–23 9
13:24–30 90
13:44 .... 59, 77, 171
13:45–46 59
13:47–50 29
15:24 115
18:27 37
18:23–27 34
18:31–35 35
20:1–2 8
22:36–40 112
24 97
24:6–7 98
24:36–40 63
24:44 97
24:44–46 97
25 .... 17, 92
25:1 100
25:14–15 92
25:14–29 95
25:21–23 93
25:24–25 93
25:27 93
26:1–2 94
28:28–30 35

Mark
2:7 69
2:9 68
2:17 68
3:1–6 71

184 *Image of God in the Parables*

(Mark continued)
4:3–20	88
4:35–36	63
5:5	63
5:19	62, 64
5:20	64
6:27	9
13	97
13:33	92

Luke
4:3–13	165
5:23	68
5:24	69
5:31–32	68, 77, 172
5:32	69
6:36	27
6:43–44	39
6:47	142
6:47–49	84, 141
7:12–15	57
8:5–15	88
8:11	89
8:15	88
10:25	114
10:27	114
10:29	29, 114
10:33	28
10:36	29
10:36–37	115
10:37	28
11:5–8	125
11:5–10	125
11:9–10	170
11:30	xi
12	166
12:2	168
12:13–14	165
12:16–21	167
12:35	92
13:6–9	40
15:4	3, 127
15:4–7	65
15:11–32	22, 74, 78, 172

(Luke continued)
15:20	75, 122
15:32	117
16:13	72, 73
16:19–20	72
16:22–23	73
16:29	73
17:12–19	65
17:14	77
17:14–16	65
18:1–8	146
18:9–14	46
18:14	151
18:18–19	128

John
2	95
2:6–10	122
6	95
6:5–14	122
7:1	4
10	4
10:4, 14	65
10:14	4, 77
10:22	4
14:6	139
14:17	20
18:38	145, 161
21	95
21:4–13	122

Romans
1:25	20
5:6–8	79
5:7–8	33
5:8	77, 124
8:38–39	96
9:13	27
9:15	27

1 Corinthians
13	113
15:3	45
15:20–28	xii

Galatians
5:19–21	39
5:22	100
5:22–23	39

2 Thessalonions
3:10	168

Hebrews
4	167, 168
11:1	159
12:2	xii

James
2:13	31
J5:7	40
5:8	102

1 Peter
1:3–5	31

2 Peter
2:2	20

1 John
1:1–3	20
4:6–8	20
4:8	112

Revelation
11:18	52
19:7	100
21:27	168

ABOUT THE AUTHOR

*A*uthor Author Stephen W. Hiemstra lives in Centreville, Virginia with Maryam, his wife of more than forty years. They have three grown children.

Stephen worked as an economist for twenty-seven years in more than five federal agencies, where he published numerous government studies, magazine articles, and book reviews. Check WorldCat.org for a complete listing.

Stephen has published a six-book, Christian spirituality series. He wrote his first book, *A Christian Guide to Spirituality* in 2014. In 2016, he wrote a second book, *Life in Tension*. In 2017, he published a memoir, *Called Along the Way*. In 2019, he published *Simple Faith*. In 2020, he published *Living in Christ*. His sixth book—*Image and Illumination*—was published in 2023.

In 2023, he began his Image of God series with the publication of *Image of God in the Parables* (2023) and *Image of the Holy Spirit and the Church* (2023). *Image of God in the Person of Jesus* (2024) completes this series.

Two books from his Christian spirituality series are available in Spanish: *Una Guía Cristiana a la Espiritualidad* (2015) and *Vida en Tensión* (2021). He also published his first book in German: *Ein Christlicher Leitfaden zur Spiritualität*

(2022).

In 2021, he published his debut novella, *Masquerade*, and rewrote it as a screenplay under the title: *Brandishing the Blue*. In 2023, he published a sequel, *The Detour*, and adapted it as a screenplay. In 2024, he published another sequel, *Christmas in Havana*, which has also been adapted as a screenplay.

Stephen published his first hardcover book, *Everyday Prayers for Everyday People* (2018). He also published an ebook compilation book, *Spiritual Trilogy*, that year.

Stephen has a Masters of Divinity (MDiv, 2013) from Gordon-Conwell Theological Seminary in Charlotte, North Carolina. His doctorate (Ph.D., 1985) is in agricultural economics from Michigan State University. He studied in Puerto Rico and in Germany and speaks Spanish and German.

Correspond with Stephen at T2Pneuma@gmail.com or follow his blog at http://www.T2Pneuma.net.

If you enjoyed *Image of God in the Parables*, please post a review online.

www.ingramcontent.com/pod-product-compliance
Lightning Source LLC
Chambersburg PA
CBHW050316120526
44592CB00014B/1935